Terrorism, Hot Spots and Conflict-Related Issues Series

Suits Against Terrorist States by Victims of Terrorism
Beatrice V. Mohoney (Editor)
2009. ISBN: 978-1-60692-835-6

Maintaining Homeland Security
Alan P. Proctor and Jason T. Waleford (Editors)
2009. ISBN: 978-1-60692-990-2

National Infrastructure: Protecting. Funding and Rebuilding
Frederick H. Lupul
2009. ISBN: 978-1-60692-369-6

Wasted Lessons of 9/11
U.S. House of Representatives
2009. ISBN: 978-1-60692-640-6

Antiterrorist Emergency Ventilation: System, Strategy and Decision-making
Xianting Li, Hao Cai and Lina Zhao
2009. ISBN: 978-1-60741-041-6

Terrorism Insurance
Miguel H. Palacios (Editor)
2009. ISBN: 978-1-60741-794-1

TERRORISM, HOT SPOTS AND CONFLICT-RELATED ISSUES SERIES

TERRORISM INSURANCE

MIGUEL H. PALACIOS
EDITOR

Nova Science Publishers, Inc.
New York

For permission to use material from this book please contact us:
Telephone 631-231-7269; Fax 631-231-8175
Web Site: http://www.novapublishers.com

Library of Congress Cataloging-in-Publication Data

Terrorism insurance / editor, Miguel H. Palacios.
p. cm.
Includes index.
ISBN 978-1-60741-794-1 (hardcover)
1. Terrorism insurance--United States. 2. Risk (Insurance)--United States. I. Palacios, Miguel H.
HG8054.5.T46 2009
368.4'8--dc22

2009028450

Published by Nova Science Publishers, Inc. ✢ New York

CONTENTS

PREFACE

This book looks at the issues involved with terrorism insurance and includes a side-by-side comparison of the previous law, the two House TRIA-extension bills, and the Senate bill that was ultimately signed by the President. Prior to the September 11, 2001 terrorist attacks, insurance covering terrorism losses was normally included in general insurance policies without additional cost to the policyholders. Following the attacks, both primary insurers and reinsurers pulled back from offering terrorism coverage. Congress responded to the disruption in the insurance market by passing the Terrorism Risk Insurance Act (TRIA) of 2002. TRIA created a temporary program to calm the insurance markets through a government backstop for terrorism losses. In addition to the continuing debate about TRIA, this book also discusses commonly accepted principles of insurability and whether nuclear, biological, chemical, or radiological (NBCR) risks are measurable and predictable and whether private insurers currently are exposed to NBCR risks and the challenges they face in pricing such risks.

Chapter 1 - Prior to the September 11, 2001 terrorist attacks, insurance covering terrorism losses was normally included in general insurance policies without additional cost to the policyholders. Following the attacks, both primary insurers and reinsurers pulled back from offering terrorism coverage. Because insurance is required for a variety of economic transactions, it was feared that a lack of insurance against terrorism loss would have a wider economic impact.

Congress responded to the disruption in the insurance market by passing the Terrorism Risk Insurance Act of 2002 (TRIA, P.L. 107-297, 116 Stat. 2322). TRIA created a temporary program, expiring at the end of 2005, to calm the insurance markets through a government backstop for terrorism losses, and to give the industry time to gather the data and create the structures and capacity necessary for private insurance to cover terrorism risk. From 2002 to 2005, terrorism insurance became widely available and largely affordable, and the insurance industry greatly expanded its financial capacity. There was, however, little apparent success on a longer term private solution and fears persisted about wider economic consequences if insurance were not available. Congress responded to the expiration of TRIA with the passage of the Terrorism Risk Insurance Extension Act (TRIEA, P.L. 109-144, 119 Stat. 2660). TRIEA extended the TRIA program until the end of 2007 while increasing the private sector exposure to terrorism risk.

The two years under the extended TRIA program were very similar to the three years under the first act. The market for terrorism insurance improved, but doubts remained as to capacity of the private sector to finance large-scale terrorism risk in the United States, as well as whether terrorism risk can be considered an insurable event at all. In response, the House passed H.R. 2761 in the 110th Congress, which would have extended the TRIA program 15 years and made substantial other changes. The Senate also passed H.R. 2761, after amending it with language from S. 2285, which would have extended TRIA seven years while making more limited changes to the underlying law. The House then passed H.R. 4299, which contained the language of the Senate-passed H.R. 2761 plus some of the provisions from the previous version of H.R. 2761. The differences between the House and Senate bills included the inclusion of group life insurance, restrictions on life insurers' use of travel in underwriting, lowering the deductible and trigger after a large terrorist attack, and the reduction of the program trigger to $50 million. The Senate, however, did not act on H.R. 4299, and the House ultimately agreed to the amended version of H.R. 2761 that was previously passed by the Senate. The President signed this bill into law on December 26, 2007.

This chapter briefly outlines the issues involved with terrorism insurance and includes a side-by-side of the previous TRIA law, the two House TRIA-extension bills, and the Senate bill that was ultimately signed by the President. It will not be updated. For more complete information on the issue, please see CRS Report RL34025, *Terrorism Risk Insurance: Issue Analysis and Legislation*, by Baird Webel.

Chapter 2 - Following the September 11, 2001 terrorist attacks, insurance protecting against property losses that might occur in future attacks became costly or unavailable for many businesses. In response, Congress passed the Terrorism Risk Insurance Act of 2002 (TRIA, P.L. 107-297, 116 Stat. 2322), creating a temporary reinsurance backstop that would spread terrorism losses over time and over a wider base of companies and policyholders while having taxpayers absorb some of these losses, particularly in the event of a large-scale terrorist attack. TRIA was limited to commercial property and casualty insurance, covering up to $100 billion each year after set insurer deductibles. The government would have paid 90% of insured losses over the deductible. If the losses were under a certain amount, ranging from $10 billion to $15 billion, the industry would have been required to pay back the government-provided funds through industry-wide recoupments.

Concern was expressed even before the enactment of TRIA that a three-year program would be too limited to allow the private sector to develop the capacity to insure terrorism risk. Responding to these concerns, the 109th Congress passed the Terrorism Risk Insurance Extension Act of 2005 (TRIEA, P.L. 109-144, 119 Stat. 2660) in December 2005. TRIEA extended the program two years, until the end of 2007, and generally reduced the government's exposure to terrorism losses. It did this by (1) excluding a number of insurance lines that had been covered; (2) increasing the minimum event size necessary for the government backstop to pay losses from $5 million to $100 million; (3) increasing the individual insurer deductibles from 15% to 20%; (4) increasing the industry's aggregate retention amount from $15 billion to $27.5 billion; and (5) reducing the government's share of losses from 90% to 85%.

As with the initial three-year TRIA, the two-year extension was considered by many to be insufficient to address adequately the challenges that arise from the need to insure against terrorism losses. Some of those seeking to further extend TRIA argue that terrorism is completely uninsurable and thus a permanent program is needed. Other TRIA supporters take the view that the private market may be able to insure against terrorism in the future, but the current TRIA program has not existed long enough to allow the private market to develop. A third point of view is that TRIA itself is stifling the development of the private market and should be further reduced, if not eliminated, to allow the development of a private market solution.

In the 110th Congress, the House passed H.R. 2761 on September 19, 2007. This bill would make substantial changes to TRIA, including adding 15 years to the program; adding group life insurance; requiring that insurers cover nuclear, biological, chemical and radiological attacks; and lowering the program trigger amount to $50 million. S. 2285, a bill that would extend the program only seven years and add domestic terrorism to the program, was reported out of committee in the Senate on November 1, 2007. This report provides an overview of TRIA-related issues, including a summary of the current TRIA program as well as the legislation that created and extended the program.

Chapter 3 - The Terrorism Risk Insurance Act of 2002 (TRIA) is credited with stabilizing insurance markets after the September 11, 2001, attacks by requiring insurers to offer terrorism coverage to commercial property owners (property/casualty insurance), and specifying that the federal government is liable for a large share of related losses. While TRIA covers attacks involving conventional weapons, insurers may use exceptions that may exclude coverage for attacks with nuclear, biological, chemical, or radiological (NBCR) weapons, which has raised concerns about the potential economic consequences of such attacks. TRIA's 2007 reauthorization directed GAO to review (1) the extent to which insurers offer NBCR coverage, (2) factors that contribute to the willingness of insurers to provide NBCR coverage, and (3) policy options for expanding coverage for NBCR risks. To do this work, GAO reviewed studies and reports and interviewed more than 100 industry participants about the availability of NBCR coverage in the market.

GAO provided a draft of this chapter to the Department of the Treasury and the National Association of Insurance Commissioners (NAIC). Treasury and NAIC said that they found the report informative and useful. NAIC did express what it said was a philosophical difference of opinion with GAO's characterization of risk-based premiums for workers' compensation insurers.

Chapter 4 - The Terrorism Risk Insurance Act of 2002 (TRIA) specifies that the federal government assume significant financial responsibility for insured losses on commercial properties resulting from future terrorist attacks. While TRIA has been credited with stabilizing markets for terrorism insurance after the September 11, 2001, attacks, questions remain as to whether certain policyholders, especially those located in large urban areas viewed as being at high risk of attack, may still face challenges in obtaining coverage. GAO was asked to conduct a study to describe (1) whether the availability of terrorism insurance for commercial properties is constrained in any geographic markets, (2) factors limiting insurers' willingness to provide coverage, and (3) advantages and disadvantages of selected public policy options to increase the availability of such insurance.

To address these objectives, GAO analyzed available data and interviewed industry participants, including those with expertise in specific geographic markets considered to be at high, moderate, or low risk of attack (Atlanta, Boston, Chicago, New York, San Francisco, and Washington, D.C.).

GAO provided a draft of this chapter to the Department of the Treasury and the National Association of Insurance Commissioners (NAIC). Treasury and NAIC said the report was informative and useful.

Chapter 5 - Terrorists using unconventional weapons, also known as nuclear, biological, chemical, or radiological (NBCR) weapons, could cause devastating losses. The Terrorism Risk Insurance Act (TRIA) of 2002, as well as the extension passed in 2005, will cover losses from a certified act of terrorism, irrespective of the weapon used, if those types of losses are included in the coverage. Because of a lack of information about the willingness of insurers to cover NBCR risks and uncertainties about the extent to which these risks can be and are being insured by private insurers across various lines of insurance, GAO was asked to study these issues. This chapter discusses (1) commonly accepted principles of insurability and whether NBCR risks are measurable and predictable, and (2) whether private insurers currently are exposed to NBCR risks and the challenges they face in pricing such risks. GAO collected information from and met with some of the largest insurers in each line of insurance, associations representing a broader cross section of the industry and state insurance regulators.

GAO makes no recommendations in this chapter.

* some discussion as to whether NBCR risks are "insurable"

In: Terrorism Insurance
Editor: Miguel H. Palacios

ISBN: 978-1-60741-794-1

Chapter 1

TERRORISM RISK INSURANCE LEGISLATION IN 2007: ISSUE SUMMARY AND SIDE-BY-SIDE

Baird Webel

SUMMARY

Prior to the September 11, 2001 terrorist attacks, insurance covering terrorism losses was normally included in general insurance policies without additional cost to the policyholders. Following the attacks, both primary insurers and reinsurers pulled back from offering terrorism coverage. Because insurance is required for a variety of economic transactions, it was feared that a lack of insurance against terrorism loss would have a wider economic impact.

Congress responded to the disruption in the insurance market by passing the Terrorism Risk Insurance Act of 2002 (TRIA, P.L. 107-297, 116 Stat. 2322). TRIA created a temporary program, expiring at the end of 2005, to calm the insurance markets through a government backstop for terrorism losses, and to give the industry time to gather the data and create the structures and capacity necessary for private insurance to cover terrorism risk. From 2002 to 2005, terrorism insurance became widely available and largely affordable, and the insurance industry greatly expanded its financial capacity. There was, however, little apparent success on a longer term private solution and fears persisted about wider economic consequences if insurance were not available. Congress responded to the expiration of TRIA with the passage of the Terrorism Risk Insurance Extension Act (TRIEA, P.L. 109-144, 119 Stat. 2660). TRIEA extended the TRIA program until the end of 2007 while increasing the private sector exposure to terrorism risk.

The two years under the extended TRIA program were very similar to the three years under the first act. The market for terrorism insurance improved, but doubts remained as to capacity of the private sector to finance large-scale terrorism risk in the United States, as well as whether terrorism risk can be considered an insurable event at all. In response, the House passed H.R. 2761 in the 110th Congress, which would have extended the TRIA program 15 years and made substantial other changes. The Senate also passed H.R. 2761, after amending it with language from S. 2285, which would have extended TRIA seven years while making more limited changes to the underlying law. The House then passed H.R. 4299, which contained the language of the Senate-passed H.R. 2761 plus some of the provisions from the previous version of H.R. 2761. The differences between the House and Senate bills included the inclusion of group life insurance, restrictions on life insurers' use of travel in underwriting, lowering the deductible and trigger after a large terrorist attack, and the reduction of the program trigger to $50 million. The Senate, however, did not act on H.R. 4299, and the House ultimately agreed to the amended version of H.R. 2761 that was previously passed by the Senate. The President signed this bill into law on December 26, 2007.

This chapter briefly outlines the issues involved with terrorism insurance and includes a side-by-side of the previous TRIA law, the two House TRIA-extension bills, and the Senate bill that was ultimately signed by the President. For more complete information on the issue, please see CRS Report RL34025, *Terrorism Risk Insurance: Issue Analysis and Legislation*, by Baird Webel.

INTRODUCTION

Prior to the September 11, 2001 terrorist attacks, insurance covering terrorism losses was normally included in general insurance policies without a specific premium being paid for this coverage. The attacks, and the more than $30 billion in insured losses that resulted from them, caused a rethinking of the possibilities of future terrorist attacks. In response to the new appreciation of the threat and the perceived inability to calculate the probability of loss and gather the loss data critical for pricing insurance, both primary insurers and reinsurers pulled back from offering terrorism coverage. Many argued that terrorism risk is essentially uninsurable by the private market due to the uncertainty and potentially massive losses involved. Because insurance is required for a variety of economic transactions, many feared that a lack of insurance against terrorism loss would have wider economic impact, particularly on large-scale developments in urban areas that would be tempting targets for terrorism.

Congress responded to the disruption in the insurance market by passing the Terrorism Risk Insurance Act of 2002 (TRIA)[1], which was signed by the President in November 2002. TRIA created the Terrorism Risk Insurance Program,[2] which was enacted as a temporary program, expiring at the end of 2005, to calm the insurance markets through a government backstop for terrorism losses and give the private industry time to gather the data and create the structures and capacity necessary for private insurance to cover terrorism risk.

Terrorism insurance became widely available under TRIA, and the insurance industry greatly expanded its financial capacity in the three years from 2002 to 2005. Less progress, however, was made on creating terrorism models that are sufficiently robust for insurers to return to offering widespread terrorism coverage without a government backstop, and practically no progress was made on a private pooling mechanism to cover terrorism risk. Again fearing economic disruption from the absence of terrorism insurance, Congress passed, and the President signed, the Terrorism Risk Insurance Extension Act of 2005 (TRIEA)[3] in December 2005. TRIEA extended the program for two years while increasing the private sector exposure under the program.

The two years' experience under TRIEA proved to be similar to the three under TRIA. During this time, terrorism risk insurance was available, pricing was moderate, and takeup rates slowly increased. Some additional progress was made on a larger scale private solution and some private groups outlined proposals for such a solution.[4] There was, however, little concrete movement towards adopting such proposals. The industry focus seemed to be on promoting the possibility of another extension of the TRIA program.

Some see this experience as proof of the argument that the private market will never be able to offer insurance to cover terrorism risk and continue to see the possibility of wider economic consequences if terrorism insurance again is unavailable. Others, notably the U.S. Treasury Department, respond that TRIA itself is retarding the growth of this private market by offering essentially free reinsurance against terrorism risk. Thus, it should be allowed to expire, or at least be reduced from its current form.

LEGISLATIVE ACTION

In the first session of the 110th Congress, three different bills addressing the impending expiration of the TRIA program saw committee or floor action, two in the House and one in the Senate. As was the case in the TRIA extension debate in 2005, the House bills were more significant revisions and expansions of the TRIA program, whereas the Senate bill had a narrower focus—extending the program while making more limited changes. Also as in 2005, the Administration generally supported the Senate's approach.

Terrorism Risk Insurance Revision and Extension Act of 2007 (TRIREA, H.R. 2761)

Representative Michael Capuano, along with 23 cosponsors, introduced H.R. 2761 on June 18, 2007. Referred to the Financial Services Committee, the bill was the subject of a hearing in that committee's Subcommittee on Capital Markets, Insurance, and Government Sponsored Enterprises on June 21, 2007.

H.R. 2761 as introduced would have extended and revised the current structure of the Terrorism Risk Insurance Program, adding significant new elements to this structure. Within the existing TRIA structure, the bill would have extended the program 10 years, to the end of 2017, while reducing the program trigger to $50 million and generally leaving the individual insurer deductibles and aggregate retention unchanged at 20% of direct earned premium and $27.5 billion, respectively. It also would have expanded the scope of TRIA by including domestic terrorism as a covered event, adding group life insurance as a covered line, and mandating that insurers make available coverage for nuclear, biological, chemical, and radiological (NCBR) terrorist events. Under the bill as introduced, group life insurance would have had a separate pool, with its own deductibles and recoupment amounts based on the amount of insurance at risk, rather than direct earned premiums. NCBR coverage would have had a lower (7.5%) deductible compared to non-NCBR terrorist events (20%). In addition, H.R. 2761 as introduced included so-called reset provisions, that would have lowered the program trigger and deductible thresholds for areas that have suffered past terrorist attacks or that suffer terrorist attacks in the future if the damage from the attacks exceeds $1 billion. Finally, the bill would have expanded the mandatory availability provisions to include restrictions on life insurers' ability to consider lawful international travel as a factor in underwriting decisions.

H.R. 2761 was marked up by the House Financial Services Committee's Subcommittee on Insurance, Capital Markets and Government Sponsored Enterprises on July 24, 2007, and by the full committee on August 1, 2007.[5] Substantial amendments were adopted at both markups. The subcommittee markup began with a complete substitute amendment by Chairman Kanjorski being adopted by voice vote. This substitute changed the NBCR provisions, delaying the make available provisions until 2009 and lowering the deductible to 3.5% with a 0.5% increase per year. It also included a requirement for biennial reporting on the TRIA program by the Treasury and changed the composition of the independent commission created by the bill to make recommendations on the program. Several amendments to reduce the 10-year extension of the program were rejected, as was one to require fullrecoupment of federal funds expended beyond the $27.5 billion aggregate retention amount in current law. Amendments adopted by the subcommittee included one by Representative Gary Ackerman to include the Secretary of Homeland Security in the certification of a terrorist attack under TRIA, and one by Representative Richard Baker to apply the lower trigger amount in the retrospective reset provisions to the entire country rather than just to the affected area.

The full committee markup began with an amendment by Chairman Barney Frank making a number of technical changes and three primary substantive changes. First, Chairman Frank's amendment changed the reset provisions, removing the retrospective reset altogether and applying the prospective reset provisions to the entire country. Thus, if there were a future terrorist attack resulting in more than $1 billion in damages, the trigger would be reduced to $5 million and the insurer deductible would be reduced to 5% for those insurers suffering terrorism losses. Second, it included temporary preemptions from state rate and form approval laws for NBCR coverage mandated under the bill. Third, it would have established a "terrorism buy down fund" in the U.S. Treasury, essentially allowing insurers to put aside reserves that would grow tax-free to cover losses from future terrorist attacks that are not reimbursed by TRIA. The U.S. Treasury could have also borrowed from this fund to cover the federal share of a future terrorist attack. The committee adopted a number of additional amendments, including: (1) an exemption for small insurers from the requirement to make NCBR coverage available; (2) the return of farmowners multiple peril as a TRIA-covered line; (3) a specific allowance for insurers to partner in meeting the requirement to make NCBR coverage available; (4) indexing various dollar amounts in the bill to an unspecified measure of inflation; (5) provision for a report by the Secretary of the Treasury in the event that the Secretary decides not to recoup expended federal funds beyond $27.5 billion; (6) extension of the program for 15 years, to the end of 2022; and (7) an increase in the post-reset deductible by 0.5% per year. The amended bill was forwarded to the full House by a vote of 49-20.

The Congressional Budget Office (CBO) issued a cost estimate for H.R. 2761 on September 6, 2007. CBO found that the bill as reported would increase direct spending by $3.7 billion from 2008 to 2012 and $10.4 billion from 2008 to 2017. This spending would be offset by additional revenues of about $100 million from 2008 to 2012 and $2.0 billion from 2008 to 2017. Since the cost estimate found that an increase in the budget deficit, or decrease in surplus, would result from the bill, it appeared to fail to meet the requirements of the "pay-as-you-go" (PAYGO) rule adopted by the House at the beginning of the 110th Congress.[6]

In response to the PAYGO issues, the special rule (H.Res. 660) under which TRIREA was considered on the House floor included a self-executing amendment that inserted language into the underlying bill requiring passage by Congress of a joint resolution before any funds could be expended. H.Res. 660 provided for expedited consideration of this future resolution, including a waiver of all points of order against it and its consideration. This requirement for future congressional action introduced uncertainty to the TRIA program that did not exist before. It was unclear exactly how the insurance market might have reacted to this uncertainty, should this language have become law.

H.R. 2761 was brought up on the House floor under H.Res. 660 on September 19, 2007. The rule made in order two floor amendments and a motion to recommit with instructions. The manager's amendment (H.Amdt. 801) by Chairman Barney Frank changed the bill to include the NBCR deductible in the reset provisions, modified the certification process for an NCBR attack, indexed the dollar amounts in the bill specifically to the Consumer Price Index for All Urban Consumers (CPIU), and made a variety of technical and conforming changes. It passed on the House floor 426-1. The other amendment (H.Amdt. 802) was offered by Representative Steve Pearce. It would have changed the increase in the deductible under the postattack reset provisions from 0.5% per year to 1% per year. This amendment failed by a vote of 194-230. The motion to recommit with instructions was offered by Representative David Drier and failed by a vote of 196-228. The House then passed the bill as amended by a vote of 312-110. H.R. 2761 was received in the Senate on September 20, 2007, read twice, and referred to the Committee on Banking, Housing, and Urban Affairs.

To summarize, H.R. 2761 as passed by the House included provisions that would have made the following changes to the current Terrorism Risk Insurance Program:

- extended the TRIA program for 15 years, until the end of 2022;
- made spending by the program contingent on passage of a future joint resolution;
- added coverage for domestic terrorist acts in the program;
- added the Secretary of Homeland Security to the certification process;
- added group life insurance to the program with a separate set of retentions and deductibles;
- returned farmowners multiple peril as a covered line;
- reduced the general trigger to $50 million;
- required insurers to cover nuclear, biological, chemical, and
- radiological (NCBR) terrorist attacks starting in 2009;
- lowered insurer deductible for NCBR attacks to 3.5% immediately and then raised that number by 0.5% per year in the future;
- increased the federal share of NCBR losses from 85% to as high as 100% for attacks causing over $100 billion in losses;
- temporarily preempted state laws on rate and form filing for NCBR coverages;
- provided the possibility of relief from NBCR requirement to smaller insurers;
- reset individual insurer deductibles to 5% and the program trigger to $5 million in the aftermath of a future terrorist attack (or series of attacks) that causes more than $1

billion in damage. Deductible reset would have been only for insurers who suffer losses.

- increased the post-reset insurer deductibles by 0.5% per year;
- established a "Terrorism Buy-Down Fund" that would have essentially allowed insurers to put aside reserves that would grow tax-free to cover future losses that are not reimbursed by TRIA. The fund would also have been available to the Secretary of the Treasury to cover the federal share of TRIA losses.
- restricted life insurers' use of foreign travel as an underwriting tool; and
- indexed the dollar amounts in the program to future inflation.

Administration Reaction to H.R. 2761. The Office of Management and Budget (OMB) released a Statement of Administration Policy on September 17, 2007, indicating that "if H.R. 2761 as reported were presented to the President, his senior advisors would recommend that he veto the bill."[7] The Administration objected to the length of term of the extension, as well as the increase in the federal role and the expansion of the scope of coverage.

Terrorism Risk Insurance Program Reauthorization Act of 2007 (TRIPRA, S. 2285)

The Senate Banking, Housing, and Urban Affairs Committee marked up this legislation as an original bill on October 17, 2007. While Senator Charles Schumer discussed possible amendments in the markup session, no amendments were voted on in committee. The unamended bill was ordered reported to the full Senate on a vote of 20-1. Chairman Christopher Dodd introduced the bill, numbered S. 2285, on November 1, 2007, and the committee report (S.Rept. 110-215) was issued the same day.

TRIPRA as introduced was a relatively straightforward reauthorization of the existing TRIA program. The two primary changes to current law were to

- extend the program for seven years, until 2014; and
- add coverage for domestic terrorist attacks to the program.

In addition, S. 2285 would have modified slightly the annual liability cap, and required the Secretary of the Treasury to promulgate regulations on determining payments, should losses exceed $100 billion rather than leaving this determination to a future Congress. The bill called for reports from the Government Accountability Office (GAO) on the possibility of insurance coverage for NCBR events (within one year) and on the affordability and availability of terrorism insurance in specific markets (within 180 days). Finally, the President's Working Group on Financial Markets was tasked to continue its analysis of the longer term availability and affordability of terrorism risk insurance, and to report on this subject in 2010 and 2013.

CBO issued a cost estimate for S. 2285 on October 29, 2007. It found that the bill would increase direct spending by $3.1 billion from 2008 to 2012 and by $6.6 billion from 2008 to 2017. This spending would be offset by increased government receipts of $100 million from 2008 to 2012 and $1.5 billion from 2008 to 2017. This score caused similar PAYGO issues as those faced in the House.[8]

In response to these PAYGO issues, language was added to TRIPRA before it was considered on the Senate floor. This new language increased the total amount of the recoupment surcharge to 133% of the previous mandatory recoupment amount. It also increased the rate of repayment — requiring that repayment be completed by September 30, 2012, for any attack before 2011, and that repayment be completed by September 30, 2017, for any attack after 2011. For any attack during 2011, 35% of the repayment must be completed by September 30, 2012, and 65% of repayment must be completed by September 30, 2017. It also removed the 3% limit on mandatory recoupment amounts.

CBO issued a cost estimate for the amended version of S. 2285 on November 15, 2007. This estimate found that, while the expected amount of direct spending would not be affected, the offsetting government receipts would be increased. In total, CBO found the amended version would reduce budget deficits or increase surpluses by less than $50 million over the 5- and 10-year windows. Thus, the amended version would not face a point of order under the PAYGO rules.

On November 16, 2006, the Senate took up the House-passed version of H.R. 2761, and amended it by unanimous consent with S.Amdt. 3800, which contained the language from the committee-passed S. 2285, plus the new language as scored by CBO. This amended version of H.R. 2761 was then passed by unanimous consent and the House was informed of the Senate action. At this time, however, the Senate did not request a conference with the House to reconcile the differences between the two versions of H.R. 2761.

Administration Reaction to the Senate Action. No official Statement of Administration Policy was released on S. 2285 or the amended version of H.R. 2761. Treasury Secretary Henry M. Paulson, however, indicated in a letter that the Administration would be willing to accept the bill as it passed the Senate committee.[9]

Terrorism Risk Insurance Program Reauthorization Act of 2007 (H.R. 4299)

With no conference committee to reconcile the versions of H.R. 2761, the House Rules Committee passed two rules (H.Res. 849 and H.Res. 862) to govern further consideration of TRIA-extension legislation. H.Res 849 provided for the consideration of the Senate-passed version of H.R. 2761 with one amendment made in order. H.Res. 862 provided for the consideration of a new bill (H.R. 4299), which was introduced by Chairman Barney Frank on December 6, 2007. H.R. 4299 consisted of the language of H.R. 2761 as passed by the Senate, plus the text of the amendment to H.R. 2761 that was made in order by H.Res. 849. The new language would have made the following changes to the Senate-passed bill:

- added coverage of group life insurance with a separate deductible, retention pool, recoupment amount, and policy surcharge amount;
- decreased the individual insurer deductible in 2008 to 5% for insurers suffering losses in terrorist attacks that exceed $1 billion, and then increase this amount by 0.5% per year after 2008;
- reset, after a $1 billion event, the trigger to $5 million, and the insurer deductible for insurers suffering losses to 5% with a 0.5% increase per year thereafter;

- restricted life insurers' use of foreign travel as an underwriting tool; and
- reduced the program trigger to $50 million.

The House considered H.R. 4299 under the provisions of H.Res. 862 on December 12, 2007. The bill passed on a vote of 303-116 and was forwarded to the Senate.

Administration Reaction to H.R. 4299. OMB released a Statement of Administration Policy on the new House language on December 7, 2007. This statement reiterated administration support for the Senate-passed bill, and indicated the House additions to this bill would result in a veto recommendation from the President's senior advisors.[10]

Final Passage and Enactment of TRIA-Extension Legislation

H.R. 4299 was referred to the Senate Banking, Housing, and Urban Affairs Committee on December 13, 2007. No action, however, was taken by the committee or the full Senate on this bill. On December 18, 2007, the House took up H.R. 2761 as previously amended by the Senate and passed this bill on a vote of 360-53. H.R. 2761 was signed by the President on December 26, 2007, becoming P.L. 110-160.

P.L. 110-160 makes the following changes to the previous law:

- The TRIA program is extended for seven years, until 2014.
- Domestic terrorist attacks are covered by the program.
- The annual liability cap language is modified, clarifying that insurers are not responsible for losses exceeding $100 billion.
- The Secretary of the Treasury is directed to provide a report within 120 days and to promulgate regulations within 240 days on determining the pro rata share of payments in the event that losses exceed $100 billion.
- The Government Accountability Office (GAO) is directed to issue reports on the possibility of insurance coverage for NCBR events (within one year) and on the affordability and availability of terrorism insurance in specific markets (within 180 days).
- The President's Working Group on Financial Markets is directed to continue its analysis of the longer term availability and affordability of terrorism risk insurance, and to report on this subject in 2010 and 2013.The total amount of the recoupment surcharge is increased to 133% of the previous mandatory recoupment amount.
- Any recoupment amount is now accelerated with the following criteria: (1) for any attack before 2011 repayment must be completed by September 30, 2012; (2) for any attack during 2011, 35% of the repayment must be completed by September 30, 2012, and 65% of repayment must be completed by September 30, 2017; and (3) for any attack after 2011 repayment must be completed by September 30, 2017.
- There is no longer a 3% limit on mandatory recoupment amounts.

Table 1. Terrorism Risk Insurance Side-by Side: Previous Law, H.R. 2761 (as passed by the House), H.R. 4299 (as passed by the House), and P.L. 110-160.

Provision	15 U.S.C. 6701 note (P.L. 107-297 *as amended by P.L. 109-144*)	H.R. 2761 (as initially passed by the House)	H.R. 4299 (as passed by the House)	P.L. 110-160 (H.R. 2761 as amended by the Senate and subsequently passed by the House)
Title	Terrorism Insurance Program	Terrorism Risk Insurance Revision and Extension Act of 2007	Terrorism Risk Insurance Program Reauthorization Act of 2007	Terrorism Risk Insurance Program Reauthorization Act of 2007
Expiration Date	December 31, 2007 (Sec. 8(a))	December 31, 2022 (Sec. 2)	December 31, 2014 (Sec. 3)	December 31, 2014 (Sec. 3)
"Act of Terrorism" Definition	For an act of terrorism to be co-vered under TRIA, it must be a violent act committed on behalf of a foreign person or interest as part of an effort to coerce the U.S. civilian population or infl-uence U.S. government policy. It must have resulted in damage within the United States or to a U.S. airliner or mission abroad. Terrorist act is to be certified by the Secretary of the Trea-sury in concurrence with the Attorney General and Secretary of State. (Sec. 102(1)(A))	Removes requirement that a covered act of terrorism be committed on behalf of a foreign person or interest. Adds "Nuclear, Biological, Chemical, and Radiological (NBCR) Terrorism" as a se-parate category of terrorism. Adds Secretary of Homeland Security to the certification of an act of terrorism or NBCR terrorism. (Sec. 102 (1))	Removes requirement that a covered act of terrorism be committed on behalf of a foreign person or interest. (Sec. 2)	Removes requirement that a covered act of terrorism be committed on behalf of a foreign person or interest. (Sec. 2)
Aggregate Industry Loss Requirement and Program Trigger	Terrorist act must cause more than $5 million in losses to be certified. *Program Trigger prevents coverage under the program unless aggregate industry losses exceed $50,000,000 in 2006 or $100,000,000 in 2007.*(Secs.102(1)(B)(ii) and 103(e)(1)(B))	Lowers Program Trigger to $50,000,000 for the life of the program. Trigger will reset to $5,000,000 after a terrorist attack resulting in $1,000,000,000 in damage. (Sec. 103 (e)(1)(C))	Lowers Program Trigger to $50,000,000 for the life of the program. Trigger will reset to $5,000,000 after a terrorist attack resulting in $1,000,000,000 in damage. (Secs. 9 and 7(2))	No Similar Provision

Table 1. (Continued)

Provision	15 U.S.C. 6701 note (P.L. 107-297 *as amended by P.L. 109-144*)	H.R. 2761 (as initially passed by the House)	H.R. 4299 (as passed by the House)	P.L. 110-160 (H.R. 2761 as amended by the Senate and subsequently passed by the House)
Insurer Deductible	7% of earned premium for 2003, 10% of earned premium for 2004, 15% of earned premium for 2005, *17.5% of earned premium for 2006, 20% of earned premium for 2007.* (Sec. 102(7))	Adds deductible for group life equal to 0.0351% of the value of an insurer's amount at risk. (Sec. 102 (11)(G)(ii)).	Lowers deducible to 5% in 2008 in the event of a terrorist attack, or series of terrorist attacks, totaling $1,000,000,000 or more for those insurers suffering damage in the attack. Raises this large event deductible 0.5% per year in future years. Adds deductible for group life equal to 0.0351% of the value of an insurer's amount at risk. (Secs. 7(1) and 6(b)(4)(A)(ii))	No Similar Provision
NBCR Deductible	No Provision	In the event of an NBCR terrorist attack, the property/casualty deductible is 3.5% the first year and then is raised 0.5% per year thereafter. The group life NBCR deductible is 0.00614% the first year and then raised 0.00088% per year thereafter. (Sec. 102(11)(I))	No Similar Provision	No Similar Provision
Reset Provisions	No Provision	In the event of a terrorist attack or series of attacks that cause more than $1,000,000,000 in damage, for future program years: (1) the Program Trigger would be reduced to $5,000,000; (2) the	In the event of a terrorist attack or series of attacks that cause more than $1,000,000,000 in damage, for future program years: (1) the Program Trigger would be reduced to $5,000,000; (2) the deductible	No Similar Provision

Table 1. (Continued)

Provision	15 U.S.C. 6701 note (P.L. 107-297 *as amended by P.L. 109-144*)	H.R. 2761 (as initially passed by the House)	H.R. 4299 (as passed by the House)	P.L. 110-160 (H.R. 2761 as amended by the Senate and subsequently passed by the House)
		deductible for any insurer suffering damage would be lowered to 5% and then be raised 0.5% per year thereafter. (Secs. 103 (e)(1)(C) and 102(11)(J))	for any insurer suffering damage would be lowered to 5% and then be raised 0.5% per year thereafter. (Sec. 7)	
NBCR Reset Provisions	No Provision	Starting with the fifth additional program year (2012), in the event of an NBCR terrorist attack or series of attacks that cause more than $1,000,000,000, the deductible for any insurer suffering losses would be lowered to 5% and then be raised 0.5% per year thereafter. (Sec. 102(11)(K))	No Similar Provision	No Similar Provision
Covered lines of Insurance	Commercial property casualty insurance including excess insurance, workers' compensa-tion, and surety but excluding crop insurance, private mortgage insurance, title insurance, financial guaranty insurance, medical malpractice insurance, health or life insurance, flood insurance, reinsurance, *comercial auto, burglary and theft, professional liability (except for directors and officers liability), and farm owners multiple peril.* (Sec. 102(12))	Adds farm owners multiple peril back to covered lines. Adds group life insurance. (Secs. 102(5), 102(8), and 102(17))	Adds group life insurance. (Sec. 6)	No Similar Provision

Table 1. (Continued)

Provision	15 U.S.C. 6701 note (P.L. 107-297 *as amended by P.L. 109-144*)	H.R. 2761 (as initially passed by the House)	H.R. 4299 (as passed by the House)	P.L. 110-160 (H.R. 2761 as amended by the Senate and subsequently passed by the House)
Mandatory Availability	Every insurer must make terrorism coverage available that does not differ materially from coverage applicable to losses other than terrorism. (Sec 103(c))	Adds coverage for NBCR terrorism to that which must be made available starting in 2009. (Sec. 103(c)) Allows for an exemption to small insurers from the requirement to provide NBCR coverage. (Sec. 103 (a)(4))	No Similar Provision	No Similar Provision
Life Insurance and Travel	No Provision	Limits life insurers from considering lawful travel in underwriting life insurance except in certain circumstances. (Sec. 103 (c)(4))	Limits life insurers from considering lawful travel in underwriting life insurance except in certain circumstances. (Sec. 8)	No Similar Provision
Insured Shared Loss Compensation	Federal share of losses is 90% for insured losses that exceed the applicable insurer deducti-ble from 2002-*2006*. *For 2007, federal share of losses is 85%.* (Sec. 103(e))	Adds sliding scale for federal share of NBCR terrorism losses, from 85% for losses less than \$10,000,000,000 to 100% for losses greater than \$100,000,000,000. (Sec. 103(e)(1)(B))	No Similar Provision	No Similar Provision
Aggregate Retention Amount Maximum	\$10,000,000,000 for 2002-3, \$12,500,000,000 for 2004, \$15,000,000,000 for 2005, *\$25,000,000,000 for 2006, \$27,500,000,000 for 2007.* (Sec. 103 (e)(6))	Adds aggregate retention amount for group life insurance equal to \$5,000,000,000. (Sec.103 (e)(7)(ii))	Adds aggregate retention amount for group life insurance equal to \$5,000,000,000. (Sec. 6(d))	No Similar Provision
Annual Liability Cap	Should losses to terrorism exceed \$100,000,000, the federal government will not make any payments on the portion of losses	Payment for federal government share would be capped at \$100,000,000,000. Assuming that an insurer has met its	Removes the possibility that a future Congress could require insurers to cover some share of losses above \$100,000,000,000	Removes the possibility that a future Congress could require insurers to cover some share of losses above \$100,000,000,000

Table 1. (Continued)

Provision	15 U.S.C. 6701 note (P.L. 107-297 *as amended by P.L. 109-144*)	H.R. 2761 (as initially passed by the House)	H.R. 4299 (as passed by the House)	P.L. 110-160 (H.R. 2761 as amended by the Senate and subsequently passed by the House)
	that exceed $100,000,000,000. Assuming that an insurer has met its dedu-ctible, insurers are not respon-sible for paying losses that ex-ceed $100,000,000,000 unless Congress acts otherwise with respect to these losses. (Sec. 103 (e)(2)	deductible, insurers are not responsible for paying losses that exceed $100,000,000,000 unless Congress acts otherwise with respect to these losses. Requires insurers to clearly disclose this to policy holders. (Sec. 103(e)(2))	if the insurer has met its individual deductible. Requires insurers to clearly disclose this to policy holders. (Sec. 4(a) and Sec. 4(d))	if the insurer has met its individual deductible. Requires insurers to clearly disclose this to policy holders. (Sec. 4(a) and Sec. 4(d))
Payment Procedures if Losses Exceed $100,000,000,000	After notice by the Secretary of the Treasury, Congress determines the procedures for payments if losses exceed $100,000,000,000. (Sec. 103 (e)(3)	Secretary of the Treasury will determine the pro rata share of insured losses to be paid by each insurer. Federal courts will have jurisdiction over claims in the event that losses exceed $100,000,000,000. (Sec. 103(e)(2), 103(e)(3)(C), and 103(e)(4)(F))	Requires Secretary of the Treasury to publish regulations regarding payments if losses exceed $100,000,000,000 within 240 days of passage. (Sec. 4(c))	Requires Secretary of the Treasury to publish regulations regarding payments if losses exceed $100,000,000,000 within 240 days of passage. (Sec. 4(c))
Mandatory Recoupment of Federal Share	If insurer losses are under the aggregate retention amount, a mandatory recoupment of the federal share of the loss will be imposed. If insurer losses are over the aggregate retention amount, such recoupment is at the discretion of the Secretary of the Treasury. (Sec. 103(e)(7))	Adds an optional report should the Secretary of the Treasury choose not to require reimbursement above the aggregate retention amount. (Sec. 103(e)(8)(D))	Increases total recoupment amount to be collected by the premium surcharges to 133% of the previously defined mandatory recoupment amount. (Sec. 4 (e)(1)(A))	Increases total recoupment amount to be collected by the premium surcharges to 133% of the previously defined mandatory recoupment amount. (Sec. 4 (e)(1)(A))
Recoupment Surcharge	Surcharge is limited to 3% of property-casualty insurance premium and may be adjusted by the Secretary to take into account	Adds limit on group life insurance recoupment surcharge of 0.053% of amount at risk. (Sec.	Removes 3% limit for man-datory surcharge. Adds limit on group life insurance recoupment discretionary	Removes 3% limit for mandatory surcharge. (Sec. 4(e)(2)(A))

Table 1. (Continued)

Provision	15 U.S.C. 6701 note (P.L. 107-297 *as amended by P.L. 109-144*)	H.R. 2761 (as initially passed by the House)	H.R. 4299 (as passed by the House)	P.L. 110-160 (H.R. 2761 as amended by the Senate and subsequently passed by the House)
	the economic impact of the surcharge on urban commercial centers, the differential risk factors related to rural areas and smaller commercial centers, and the various exposures to terrorism risk across lines of insurance. (Sec. 103(8))	103(9)(C))	surcharge of 0.053% of amount at risk. (Secs. 4(e)(2)(A) and 6(g)(2))	
Timing of Mandatory Recoupment	No Provision	No provision	Requires expedited collection of recoupment amounts: (1) for a terrorist attack be-fore 2011, all required recou-pment amounts must be coll-ected by September 30, 2012; (2) for a terrorist attack in 2011, 35% of required reco-upment amounts must be co-llected by September 30, 2012, and the balance must be collected by September 30, 2017; (3) for a terrorist attack after 2011, all required recoup-ment amounts must be coll-ected by September 30, 2017. (Sec. 4(e)(1)(B))	Requires expedited collection of recoupment amounts: (1) for a terrorist attack be-fore 2011, all required recoupment amounts must be collected by September 30, 2012; (2) for a terrorist attack in 2011, 35% of required reco-upment amounts must be collected by September 30, 2012, and the balance must be collected by September 30, 2017; (3) for a terrorist attack after 2011, all required recoup-ment amounts must be coll-ected by September 30, 2017. (Sec. 4(e)(1)(B))
Joint Resolution Requirement for Future Payments	No Provision	Requires passage of a future Joint Resolution before any funds would be expended under the act. Provides for expedited consideration of this Resolution. (Sec. 103(h))	No Similar Provision	No Similar Provision

Table 1. (Continued)

Provision	15 U.S.C. 6701 note (P.L. 107-297 *as amended by P.L. 109-144*)	H.R. 2761 (as initially passed by the House)	H.R. 4299 (as passed by the House)	P.L. 110-160 (H.R. 2761 as amended by the Senate and subsequently passed by the House)
Preservation and Preemption of Existing State Law	Preserves all existing regulat-ory authority and jurisdiction of the states except that: exclusions for terrorism existing at the time of the act's enactment are annulled, but can be reinstated by the insurer with the agreement of the insured; the definition for "Act of Terrorism" in the act shall pre-empt any state definitions for purposes of the act, state rate and form filing requirements until the end of 2003 are partially preempted; and insurers are required to provide books and records relevant to the pro-gram at the request of the Sec-retary of the Treasury notwith-standing any state laws to the contrary. (Sec. 105 and 106(a))	Preempts state laws requiring prior approval of rates and forms for insurance required by the act until December 31, 2008. Preempts state laws re-quiring prior approval of forms for NBCR insurance required by the act until Dec-ember 31, 2009. Preempts state laws requiring prior approval of rates for NBCR insurance required by the act until December 31, 2010. (Sec. 3(a)(4))	No Similar Provision	No Similar Provision
Inflation Adjustment	No Provision	Indexes dollar amounts in the bill for inflation using the CPI-U as an adjustor. (Sec. 103(h))	No Similar Provision	No Similar Provision
Terrorism Buy-Down Fund	No Provision	Creates a "Terrorism Buy-Down Fund" that would allow insurers to buy additional terrorism coverage from the government. This cover-age would be limited to the amount of an insurer's dedu-ctible and co-share. Payout	No Similar Provision	No Similar Provision

Table 1. (Continued)

Provision	15 U.S.C. 6701 note (P.L. 107-297 *as amended by P.L. 109-144*)	H.R. 2761 (as initially passed by the House)	H.R. 4299 (as passed by the House)	P.L. 110-160 (H.R. 2761 as amended by the Senate and subsequently passed by the House)
		amounts would be limited to the amount that the insurer paid for the coverage plus interest. Amounts in this buy-down fund would be available to be borrowed by the Secretary of the Treasury to cover the federal share of terrorism losses should they not be needed by the insurer who purchased the coverage. (Sec. 106A)		
Studies and Reports	Calls for a study of the need to include group life insurance under TRIA (Sec. 103 (h)), a study and report of the potential impact of terrorism on life insurance and other lines of insurance (Sec 103 (g)), and a study assessing the effective-ness of the program, the likely-hood of the private industry insuring against terrorism after the program expiration, and the availability and affordability of such insurance. (Sec. 108(d)) *Calls for an analysis and re-port, not later than September 30, 2006, from the President's Working Group on Financial Markets, in consultation with various stakeholders, on the*	Calls for ongoing analysis by the Secretary of the Treasury of terrorism risk insurance market conditions and biennial reports and testimony. (Sec. 5(a))	Calls for GAO studies and reports on insurance for nuclear, biological, chemical, and radiological events and on the availability and affordability of terrorism risk insurance in specific markets. Calls for ongoing analysis by the President's Working Group on Financial Markets, with reports to be delivered in 2010 and 2013. (Sec. 5)	Calls for GAO studies and reports on insurance for nuclear, biological, chemical, and radiological events and on the availability and affordability of terrorism risk insurance in specific markets. Calls for ongoing analysis by the President's Working Group on Financial Markets, with reports to be delivered in 2010 and 2013. (Sec. 5)

Table 1. (Continued)

Provision	15 U.S.C. 6701 note (P.L. 107-297 *as amended by P.L. 109-144*)	H.R. 2761 (as initially passed by the House)	H.R. 4299 (as passed by the House)	P.L. 110-160 (H.R. 2761 as amended by the Senate and subsequently passed by the House)
	longer term availability and affordability of terrorism risk insurance including particularly group life coverage			
Commission on Terrorism Risk Insurance	No Provision	Establishes a 21-member commission with a wide range of stakeholders, including insurers, policyholders, and the insurance commissioners. The commission is to make recommendations regarding possible actions to encourage private insurance coverage of terrorism risk. The commission is to make two reports specifically evaluating the need for the TRIA program and suggesting possible replacements. One report to be submitted before 60 months after enactment and the other submitted before 96 months after enactment. (Sec. 109)	No Similar Provision	No Similar Provision

Notes: Items in *italics* under the15 U.S.C. 6701 note column are those added by P.L. 109-144. H.R. 2761 as passed by the House would strike most of 15 U.S.C. 6701 note and replace it with a similar structure, including identical language in many sections. The section numbers for this bill cited in this side-by-side are, therefore, those that would appear in the code if the bill were enacted, except for the provisions entitled "Expiration Date" and "Preservation and Preemption of Existing State Law." In contrast, the Senate-passed H.R. 2761, which became P.L. 110-160, and H.R. 4299 simply amend 15 U.S.C. 6701 note. The section numbers cited in this side-by-side are thus those of the two bills themselves.

End Notes

[1] P.L. 107-297, 116 Stat. 2322. See CRS Report RS21444, *The Terrorism Risk Insurance Act of 2002: A Summary of Provisions*, by Baird Webel.

[2] The original statute specifies the name as the "Terrorism Insurance Program" while the Department of Treasury entitles it the "Terrorism Risk Insurance Program" (TRIP) and this name has become more generally accepted.

[3] P.L. 109-144, 119 Stat. 2660. See CRS Report RL33177, *Terrorism Risk Insurance Legislation in 2005: Issue Summary and Side-by-Side*, by Baird Webel.

[4] *See*, for example, the testimony of Edmund F. Kelly before a joint hearing of the House Financial Services Subcommittees on Capital Markets, Insurance, and Government Sponsored Enterprises and Oversight and Investigations on September 7, 2006, available at [http://financialservices.house.gov/media/pdf/092706efk.pdf], visited on Jan. 14, 2008.

[5] The full committee markup began on July 26, but H.R. 2761 was the last of a number of bills to be marked up.

[6] *See* CRS Report RL33850, *The House's "Pay-As-You-Go*" (PAYGO) *Rule in the 110th Congress: A Brief Overview*, by Robert Keith, for more information on PAYGO.

[7] *See* [http://www.whitehouse.gov/omb/legislative/sap/110-1/hr2761sap-r.pdf], visited on Jan. 14, 2008.

[8] *See* CRS Report RL31943, *Budget Enforcement Procedures: Senate's Pay-As-You-Go (PAYGO) Rule*, by Bill Heniff, Jr., for more information on the Senate PAYGO rule.

[9] Relevant text of this letter was provided to CRS by the Department of the Treasury. This was also reported in the press. See [http://www.politico.com/news/stories/1007/6394.html], visited on Jan. 14, 2008.

[10] See [http://www.whitehouse.gov/omb/legislative/sap/110-1/hr2761sap-h.pdf], visited on Jan. 14, 2008.

In: Terrorism Insurance
Editor: Miguel H. Palacios

ISBN: 978-1-60741-794-1

Chapter 2

TERRORISM RISK INSURANCE: ISSUE ANALYSIS AND LEGISLATION

Baird Webel

SUMMARY

Following the September 11, 2001 terrorist attacks, insurance protecting against property losses that might occur in future attacks became costly or unavailable for many businesses. In response, Congress passed the Terrorism Risk Insurance Act of 2002 (TRIA, P.L. 107-297, 116 Stat. 2322), creating a temporary reinsurance backstop that would spread terrorism losses over time and over a wider base of companies and policyholders while having taxpayers absorb some of these losses, particularly in the event of a large-scale terrorist attack. TRIA was limited to commercial property and casualty insurance, covering up to $100 billion each year after set insurer deductibles. The government would have paid 90% of insured losses over the deductible. If the losses were under a certain amount, ranging from $10 billion to $15 billion, the industry would have been required to pay back the government-provided funds through industry-wide recoupments.

Concern was expressed even before the enactment of TRIA that a three-year program would be too limited to allow the private sector to develop the capacity to insure terrorism risk. Responding to these concerns, the 109th Congress passed the Terrorism Risk Insurance Extension Act of 2005 (TRIEA, P.L. 109-144, 119 Stat. 2660) in December 2005. TRIEA extended the program two years, until the end of 2007, and generally reduced the government's exposure to terrorism losses. It did this by (1) excluding a number of insurance lines that had been covered; (2) increasing the minimum event size necessary for the government backstop to pay losses from $5 million to $100 million; (3) increasing the individual insurer deductibles from 15% to 20%; (4) increasing the industry's aggregate retention amount from $15 billion to $27.5 billion; and (5) reducing the government's share of losses from 90% to 85%.

As with the initial three-year TRIA, the two-year extension was considered by many to be insufficient to address adequately the challenges that arise from the need to insure against terrorism losses. Some of those seeking to further extend TRIA argue that terrorism is completely uninsurable and thus a permanent program is needed. Other TRIA supporters take the view that the private market may be able to insure against terrorism in the future, but the current TRIA program has not existed long enough to allow the private market to develop. A third point of view is that TRIA itself is stifling the development of the private market and should be further reduced, if not eliminated, to allow the development of a private market solution.

In the 110th Congress, the House passed H.R. 2761 on September 19, 2007. This bill would make substantial changes to TRIA, including adding 15 years to the program; adding group life insurance; requiring that insurers cover nuclear, biological, chemical and radiological attacks; and lowering the program trigger amount to $50 million. S. 2285, a bill that would extend the program only seven years and add domestic terrorism to the program, was reported out of committee in the Senate on November 1, 2007. This chapter provides an overview of TRIA-related issues, including a summary of the current TRIA program as well as the legislation that created and extended the program.

BACKGROUND

Prior to the September 2001 attacks on the United States, insurers generally did not exclude or separately charge for terrorism risks. The events of September 11, 2001, however, changed this, as insurers realized the extent of possible terrorism losses. Estimates of insured losses from the 9/11 attacks are around $35 billion in current dollars, the largest man-made insurance disaster on record. These insured losses were concentrated in the following lines: business interruption (33% of the losses), property (30%), and liability (23%).[1]

While primary insurance companies, those who actually sell and service the insurance policies bought by consumers, certainly lost significant amounts of money, the heaviest insured losses were absorbed by foreign and domestic reinsurers — the insurers of insurance companies. Due to the lack of data on, or modeling of, terrorism risk, reinsurers felt unable to price for such risks and largely withdrew from the market for terrorism risk insurance. Once reinsurers stopped offering coverage for terrorism risk, primary insurers, also suffering from a lack of data and models, also withdrew, or tried to withdraw, from the market. In most states, state regulators must approve policy form changes, and state regulators generally agreed to insurer requests to exclude terrorism risks from their commercial policies, just as they had long excluded war risks. Terrorism risk insurance was soon unavailable or extremely expensive, and many businesses were no longer able to purchase insurance that would protect them in future terrorist attacks. Although most of the evidence is anecdotal, this problem is thought to pose a threat of serious harm to the real estate, transportation, construction, energy, and utility sectors, in turn threatening the broader economy.

Insurability of Terrorism Risk

Stripped to its most basic elements, insurance is a fairly straightforward operation. An insurer agrees to assume an indefinite future risk in exchange for a definite current premium from a consumer. The insurer pools a large number of risks such that at any given point in time, the ongoing losses will not be larger than the current premiums being paid, plus the residual amount of past premiums that the insurer retains and invests, plus, in a last resort, any borrowing against future profits if this is possible. For the insurer to operate successfully and avoid bankruptcy, it is critical to accurately estimate the probability of a loss and the severity of that loss so that a sufficient premium can be charged. Insurers generally depend upon huge databases of past loss information in setting these rates. Everyday occurrences, such as automobile accidents or natural deaths, can be estimated with great accuracy. Extraordinary events, such as large hurricanes, are more difficult, but insurers have many years of weather data coupled with sophisticated computer models with which to make predictions.

Terrorism risk, however, is seen by many to be so fundamentally different than other risks as to be essentially uninsurable by the private insurance market, and thus requires a government solution. The argument that terrorism risk is uninsurable typically focuses on lack of data about both the probability and severity of terrorist action. The reason for the lack of data is generally comforting to our nation — very few terrorist attacks have succeeded. This, however, does not assuage the fiduciary duty of an insurance company president not to put a company at risk by insuring against an event that too easily could bankrupt the firm. As a replacement for large amounts of historical data, insurers turn to various forms of models similar to those used to assess future hurricane losses. Even the best model, however, can only partly replace good data, and terrorism models are certainly still in their infancy.

One prominent insurance textbook identifies four ideal elements of an insurable risk: (1) a sufficiently large number of insureds to make the losses reasonably predictably; (2) the loss must be definite and measurable; (3) the loss must be fortuitous or accidental; and (4) the loss must not be catastrophic (i.e., it must be unlikely to produce loss to a large percentage of the risks at the same time).[2] Terrorism risk in the United States certainly fails the first criterion. It also likely fails the third due to the malevolent human actors behind terrorist attacks. Whether or not it fails the fourth criterion is largely decided by the underwriting actions of insurers themselves (i.e., whether the insurers insure a large number of risks in a single geographic area that would be affected by a terrorist strike). Unsurprisingly, insurers generally have sought to limit their exposures in particular geographic locations, making terrorism insurance more difficult to find.

International Experience with Terrorism Risk Insurance

Although the U.S. experience with terrorism is relatively limited, other countries have dealt with the issue much more extensively and have developed their own responses to the challenges presented by terrorism risk. Spain, which has seen significant terrorist activity by Basque separatist movements, has included terrorism in a broader government-owned reinsurer dealing with catastrophes since 1954. The United Kingdom, responding the Irish Republican Army attacks in the 1980s, created Pool Re, a privately owned mutual insurance company with government backing, specifically to insure terrorism risk. In the aftermath of the September 11, 2001 attacks, many foreign countries reassessed their terrorism risk and created a variety of approaches to deal with the risk. The UK greatly expanded PoolRe, while Germany created a private primary insurer with government backing to offer terrorism insurance policies. Germany's plan, as with TRIA in the United State, is a temporary measure. It is set to expire at the end of 2007 and no decision on renewal has been reached. Not all countries, however, concluded that some sort of government backing was necessary for terrorism insurance. Canada specifically considered, and rejected, creating some sort of government program following September 11, 2001, and has not changed this position, even after attempted terrorist attacks on Canada itself.

Previous U.S. Experience with "Uninsurable" Risks

Terrorism risk post-2001 is certainly not the first time that United States has faced a risk perceived as uninsurable that Congress chooses to confront. During World War II, for example Congress created a "war damage" insurance program, and there are current programs insuring against aviation and flood losses. The closest previous analog to the situation with terrorism risk is probably the federal riot reinsurance program created in the late 1960s.

Following large scale riots in American cities in the late 1960s, insurers generally pulled back from insuring in those markets, either adding policy exclusions to limit their exposure to damage from riots or ceasing to sell property damage insurance altogether. In response, Congress created a riot reinsurance program as part of the Housing and Urban Development Act of 1968.[3] The federal riot reinsurance program offered reinsurance contracts similar to commercial excess reinsurance. The federal government agreed to cover some percentage of an insurance company's losses above a certain deductible in exchange for a premium paid by that insurance company. Private reinsurers eventually returned to the market and the federal riot reinsurance program was terminated in 1985.

The Terrorism Insurance Market and the Economy: Post-9/11 and Pre-TRIA

The September 2001 terrorist attacks, and the resulting billions of dollars in insured losses, caused significant upheaval in the insurance market. Even before the attacks, the insurance market was showing signs of a cyclical "hardening" of the market in which prices typically rise and availability is somewhat limited. The unexpectedly large losses caused by terrorist action certainly exacerbated this trend. More directly, the attacks had a specific impact on the commercial lines of insurance most at risk for terrorism losses. Post-September 11 insurers and reinsurers began either including substantial surcharges for terrorism risk, or, more commonly, they excluded coverage for terrorist attacks altogether. Reinsurers could take these steps rapidly because reinsurance contracts and rates are generally unregulated. Primary insurance contracts and rates, however, are more closely regulated by the individual states and the exclusion of terrorism coverage for the individual purchaser of insurance thus required regulatory approval at the state level in most cases. States acted fairly quickly, and, in the fall of 2001, 45 states approved insurance policy language excluding terrorism damage in standard commercial policies.

The lack of readily available terrorism insurance caused fears of a larger economic impact, particularly on the real estate market. In most cases, lenders prefer, if not require, that a borrower maintain insurance coverage on a property. Lack of terrorism insurance could lead to defaults on existing loans and a downturn in future lending, causing economic ripple effects as buildings are not built and construction workers remain idle. The 14-month period after the September 2001 terrorist attacks and before the November 2002 passage of TRIA provides some insight into the effects of a lack of terrorism insurance. Some examples in September 2002 include the Real Estate Round Table, releasing a survey that "found $15.5 billion of real estate projects in 17 states were stalled or cancelled because of a continuing scarcity of terrorism insurance"[4] and Moody's Investors Service downgrading $4.5 billion in commercial mortgage-backed securities.[5] This picture, however, was not uniform. For example, in July 2002, the *Wall Street Journal* reported that "despite concerns over landlords' ability to get terrorism insurance, trophy properties were in demand."[6]

Initial Congressional Action

Congressional action to address the perceived broad economic threat from a lack of terrorism insurance began when the House Committee on Financial Services held a hearing in September 2001. Following this, its Subcommittee on Capital Markets, Insurance, and Government Sponsored Enterprises held another in October 2001. Chairman Michael Oxley introduced H.R. 3210 in the 107th Congress in November 2001. During the November 29 debate on the bill, the House accepted a substitute bill by a narrow vote. The bill provided for a temporary government loan to insurers in case of acts of terrorism; it also contained controversial provisions on litigation management.

The legislation subsequently stalled over the tort provisions. In the Senate, four bills were introduced in 2001, but the chamber took no action. In June 2002, Senators Christopher Dodd, Harry Reid, Paul Sarbanes, and Charles Schumer introduced a compromise proposal, S. 2600, which passed the Senate in July 2002. As passed, it did not require insurers to repay all federal assistance or contain the controversial liability reform.

The reconciling November 2002 conference report retained bill number H.R. 3210 and was subsequently passed. The President signed TRIA on November 26, 2002.[7]

TRIA's Original Goals and Substance

Can be used for conclusive points about effectiveness of Govt scheme

TRIA's stated goals were to (1) create a temporary federal program of shared public and private compensation for insured losses to allow the private market to stabilize; (2) protect consumers by ensuring the availability and affordability of insurance for terrorism risks; and (3) preserve state regulation of insurance.

To meet the first goal, TRIA began a short-term program for the federal government to share insured commercial property-casualty losses with the private insurance market. The program extended from enactment through December 31, 2005. The role of federal loss sharing depended on the size of the insured loss. For a small loss, there was no federal sharing. For a medium-sized loss, the federal role was to spread the loss over time and over the entire insurance industry, paying claims up-front but then recouping the payments through a broad levy on insurance policies afterwards. For a large loss, the federal government was to pay most of the losses, although recoupment was possible in these circumstances as well.

The precise criteria under TRIA were as follows: (1) the federal government would have shared in any insurer's losses only if the industry's aggregate insured losses from an act of terrorism exceeded $5 million; and (2) each insurer would have been responsible for paying out a certain amount in claims — known as its deductible — before it could call upon federal assistance. Its deductible was directly proportionate to a particular insurer's size, rising from 7% of earned premiums in 2003, to 11% in 2004, and 15% in 2005. Once these two thresholds were passed, the federal government would have paid 90% of each insurer's losses above its deductible. If, however, the aggregate industry loss had been below $10 billion for the year 2003, $12.5 billion for 2004, or $15 billion in 2005, the amount that would have been paid to individual insurers was required to be recouped through a surcharge added to all commercial insurance premiums in following years. This surcharge could be a maximum of 3% of premium and would last until the federal share was repaid. If the aggregate industry loss was greater than the $10 billion - $15 billion amount, then the law imposed no mandatory recoupment surcharge, although the Treasury Secretary was given the authority to impose such a surcharge. The maximum amount that could be paid out under the program in a given year was $100 billion.

The act covered only U.S. commercial property-casualty insured losses due to acts of international terrorism certified by the Treasury Secretary. It did not cover losses due to acts of war declared by Congress, except workers' compensation losses. Congress also "carved out" certain lines, disallowing their coverage under TRIA. The carved-out lines were federal crop insurance, private crop or livestock insurance, private mortgage insurance, title insurance, financial guaranty insurance of single-line guaranty insurers, medical malpractice, flood insurance, reinsurance, and all life insurance products.

TRIA addressed the second goal, to protect consumers, by nullifying all commercial terrorism exclusions in force on TRIA's date of enactment. TRIA required property-casualty insurers, as a condition of receiving federal assistance, to make terrorism insurance available prospectively to their commercial policyholders by February 23, 2003. The coverage could not differ materially from coverage for other types of losses. Each offer must reveal both the premium charged for terrorism insurance and the federal share of compensation. TRIA in effect gave policyholders coverage for terrorism risk immediately, without charge, until the policyholder accepted or declined the coverage TRIA required insurers to offer. The policyholder was not, however, required to purchase coverage. If the policyholder declined to do so, its insurer could exclude terrorism losses. TRIA did not limit what insurers could charge for terrorism risk insurance, though it did give state regulators the authority to modify excessive, inadequate, or unfairly discriminatory rates. The legislation made this "make available" provision effective until the end of 2004, with the Treasury Secretary having the option to continue it until the end of 2005.

TRIA's third goal was to preserve state regulation of insurance. Section 106 did so expressly, with some exceptions. One exception was the definition of an "act of terrorism": TRIA's definition applied despite any other definition in state law. A second exception was TRIA's limited preemption of state rate and form filing requirements. TRIA preempted all prior approvals through December 31, 2003, though it did allow states to invalidate an excessive or discriminatory rate and to review policy forms after their use. Thus, states retained considerable authority over rates and terms for terrorism coverage. A third exception was TRIA's requirement that workers' compensation coverage include not only coverage for terrorism risk but also for war risk. Finally, TRIA directed the Treasury Secretary to consult with the state regulators' group, the National Association of Insurance Commissioners, on several application issues.

In addition to the determination on the "make available" provisions, Congress directed the Treasury Secretary to conduct an expedited study of whether the TRIA program should be extended to group life insurance and allowed the secretary to extend TRIA to group life if the study determined that it should be. TRIA also directed the secretary to "study the potential effects of acts of terrorism on the availability of life insurance and other lines of insurance coverage, including personal lines," by August 2003. Finally, the secretary required a report to Congress by June 30, 2005, on the effectiveness of the program, the ability of the property-casualty industry to offer terrorism insurance after the program ends, and the "availability and affordability of such insurance for various policyholders, including railroads, trucking, and public transit."

Post-TRIA Activity

Executive Branch

The Treasury issued guidelines and rules for carrying out TRIA and carried out most of the studies and made determinations as directed by Congress.[8] Three Treasury actions drew the most congressional attention and controversy. In August 2003, the results of its study on group life insurance were announced, and the determination was made that group life not be covered under TRIA because such insurance was still readily available from primary insurers in the private market. This determination would have been overturned by several TRIA extension bills, but it was not overturned by the legislation that ultimately was passed. In June 2004, Treasury made the determination that the "make available" provisions should be extended through the end of the program in 2005, a determination that drew support from most in Congress.

On June 30, 2005, the Treasury issued its report on TRIA with Treasury Secretary John Snow's accompanying letter recommending against continuation of TRIA "in its present form."[9] The Secretary stressed two factors: the economy had become more robust since 9/11, and extension of TRIA would hinder the development of private insurance solutions by crowding out innovation and capacity building. To gain support from the Secretary, the letter specified that any TRIA extension should include an increase of the event threshold from $5 million to $500 million, increases in deductibles and co-payments, and a reduction in the types of insurance covered by TRIA. These requirements differ substantially from previously introduced legislation on the topic, particularly the increase to $500 million and the reduction in the types of insurance.

Terrorism Insurance Market after TRIA

The "make available" provisions of TRIA addressed the availability problem that had plagued the terrorism insurance market, as insurers were required by law to offer terrorism coverage. There was significant uncertainty, however, as to how consumers would react, since there was no consumer requirement to purchase terrorism coverage, and the pricing of terrorism coverage was initially high. Initial consumer reaction to the terrorism coverage offers was not overwhelming. Marsh, Inc., a major insurance broker, reports that only 27% of their clients bought terrorism insurance in 2003. This take-up rate, however, climbed to 49% in 2004 and 58% in 2005.[10] The take-up rates varied significantly among industries, with the highest rates seen in real estate and financial services (79% in 2005) and the lowest rates in construction and manufacturing (43% in 2005).[11] Rates also varied significantly across the country — 67% in the Northeast, 58% in the Midwest, 53% in the West, and 50% in the South.[12] Similar numbers are reported by others in the insurance market. Aon, another major insurance broker, reports an overall take-up rate of 59.3% in 2004-2005, with highest rates reported in the real estate and financial services industry (nearly 90%). Aon reported, however, that the highest take-up rate was in the South (nearly 75%) while the Northeast was much lower (nearly 55%).[13]

The price for terrorism insurance has generally declined since the aftermath of the 2001 terrorist attacks. For example, a 2005 survey by the Department of the Treasury found that the terrorism premium as a percent of the overall insurance premium was nearly 4% in 2002, and fell to slightly under 3% in 2003 and then rose to slightly over 3% in 2004. For those in high risk cities, it was approximately 6% in 2002, 5% in 2003 and slightly under 3% in 2004.[14] Marsh reported that the median premium for terrorism was 4.7% of the overall insurance premium in 2004 and 4.2% in 2005.[15]

Congressional Action in the 108th and 109th Congresses

Oversight and Hearings. Congressional oversight continued after enactment, with hearings in both the House and the Senate in April and May 2004. The principal points of concern expressed in these hearings were Treasury's prior decision to exclude group life insurance from coverage under TRIA, the thenupcoming Treasury decision on the "make available" provisions, and the possibility of a general extension of the act past its scheduled sunset date. Some concerns about TRIA extension were also raised at the hearings, and whether all who expressed support for TRIA extension agreed on the exact form of this extension was unclear as well. Officials at the Treasury Department had previously indicated repeatedly that they expect the program to expire as the law provides. When pressed for the Bush Administration's then current position on TRIA extension at the hearings, the Treasury witnesses generally indicated no strong position, preferring instead to wait for the results of the then ongoing study (issued on June 30, 2005, and discussed above).

Through the early part of the 109th Congress, many Members and interest groups seemed to be waiting for the Treasury report that was expected to provide the Administration's position on possible TRIA extension. The Senate Banking, Housing, and Urban Affairs Committee did hold a general oversight hearing on TRIA on April 14, 2005. Shortly after the release of the Treasury study, both the House (July 13, 2005) and the Senate (July 14, 2005) held hearings featuring Secretary Snow explaining further the Administration's position on TRIA extension outlined in his June 30, 2005 letter. The House Subcommittee on Capital Markets, Insurance and Government Sponsored Enterprises went further, inviting regulators, insurers and other interested parties to testify at a hearing entitled "The Future of Terrorism Insurance" on July 27, 2005.

TRIA Extension Legislation. Two bills, S. 467 and H.R. 4313, were reported out of committee to extend and revise TRIA in the 109th Congress. Different versions of S. 467 passed both the Senate and the House by early December 2005.[16]

S. 467 was introduced in the 109th Congress by Senator Christopher Dodd on February 18, 2005, prior to the Treasury report. It was marked up in the Senate Banking, Housing, and Urban Affairs Committee on November 16, 2005. The committee amended the bill substantially before reporting it favorably. S. 467, as reported, extended the program by two years and left the framework largely intact, while further limiting federal government exposure, as suggested by Treasury Secretary Snow. Specifically, it (1) removed additional of types of insurance (commercial auto, burglary and theft, surety, farm owners multiple peril, and professional liability, except for directors and officers liability); (2) raised the insurer deductible to 17.5% in 2006 and 20% in 2007; (3) increased the insurer co-payment from 10% to 15% for 2007; and (4) raised the event trigger to $50 million in 2006 and $100 million in 2007. After markup, the bill was brought to the Senate floor and passed by unanimous consent on November 18.

H.R. 4314 was introduced by Representative Richard Baker on November 14, 2005, and marked up by the House Financial Services Committee on November 16. Relatively minor amendments were made in committee, including language prohibiting life insurers from denying coverage due to lawful travel undertaken by individuals. H.R. 4314, as reported, extended TRIA and revised the program extensively. It limited the types of insurance covered by removing commercial auto, but it expanded the program to cover domestic terrorist events. Also, it increased the types of insurance covered to include group life and specific coverage for nuclear, biological, chemical, and radiological (NBCR) events. It raised the event trigger to $50 million in 2006 and an additional $50 million for every future year the program is in effect. It also changed the insurer deductible, but did so differently for different lines of insurance, raising the deductible to as much as 25% for casualty insurance but lowering it to 7.5% for NBCR events. H.R. 4314 would have raised the insurer co-payment to 20% for events under $10 billion while lowering it gradually to 5% for events over $40 billion. In the event of a terrorist attack, the deductibles and event triggers would reset to lower levels, with deductibles possibly as low as 5% in the event of a large attack. It removed the cap on the mandatory recoupment provision so that all money expended under TRIA would be recouped by the federal government through a surcharge on insurers in the years after the attack. H.R. 4314 also would have created TRIA Capital Reserve Funds (CRF), which would allow in surers to set aside untaxed reserves to tap in the case of a terrorist attack. The majority of the text of H.R. 4314 was inserted into S. 467, and the House passed this bill on December 7, 2005.

Although the House called for a conference committee reconciling the differences between the two bills, the Senate did not. Ultimately, a further amendment to S. 467, S.Amdt. 2689, passed the Senate on December 16, 2005, and the House followed, passing S. 467 as amended on December 17, 2005. The President signed the bill into P.L. 109-144 on December 22, 2005.

P.L. 109-144 closely tracks the Senate version of S. 467. The only substantial difference is an increase of the aggregate industry retention amount from $17.5 billion and $20 billion to $25 billion and $27.5 billion for 2006 and 2007.

Current Congressional Action

With the extended TRIA set to expire at the end of 2007, many in Congress have called for further legislation to reauthorize the program. Both Chairman Christopher Dodd of the Senate Banking, Housing, and Urban Affairs Committee and Chairman Barney Frank of the House Financial Services Committee indicated early in the session that terrorism insurance legislation was a high priority for their committees in the 110th Congress. The Senate Banking, Housing, and Urban Affairs Committee held a hearing on February 28, 2007, entitled "Examining the Terrorism Risk Insurance Program," and the House Financial Services Subcommittee on Capital Markets, Insurance, and Government Sponsors Enterprises held two hearings: "The Need to Extend the Terrorism Risk Insurance Act" in New York City on March 5, 2007, and "Policy Options for Extending the Terrorism Risk Insurance Act" on April 24, 2007.

Terrorism Risk Insurance Revision and Extension Act of 2007 (TRIREA)

Representative Michael Capuano, along with 23 cosponsors, introduced H.R. 2761 on June 18, 2007. Referred to the Financial Services Committee, the bill was the subject of a hearing in that committee's Subcommittee on Capital Markets, Insurance, and Government Sponsored Enterprises on June 21, 2007.

H.R. 2761 as introduced would have extended and revised the current structure of the Terrorism Risk Insurance Program, adding significant new elements to this structure. Within the existing TRIA structure, the bill would have extended the program 10 years, to the end of 2017, while reducing the program trigger to $50 million and generally leaving the individual insurer deductibles and aggregate retention unchanged at 20% of direct earned premium and $27.5 billion, respectively. It also would have expanded the scope of TRIA by including domestic terrorism as a covered event, adding group life insurance as a covered line, and mandating that insurers make available coverage for NBCR terrorist events. Under the bill as introduced, group life insurance would have had a separate pool, with its own deductibles and recoupment amounts based on the amount of insurance at risk, rather than direct earned premiums. NBCR coverage would have had a lower (7.5%) deductible compared to non-NBCR terrorist events (20%). In addition, H.R. 2761 as introduced included so-called reset provisions, that would have lowered the program thresholds for areas that have suffered past terrorist attacks or that suffer terrorist attacks in the future if the damage from the attacks exceeds $1 billion. Finally, the bill would have expanded the mandatory availability provisions to include restrictions on life insurers' ability to consider lawful international travel as a factor in underwriting decisions.

H.R. 2761 was marked up by the House Financial Services Committee's Subcommittee on Insurance, Capital Markets and Government Sponsored Enterprises on July 24, 2007, and by the full committee on August 1, 2007.[17] Substantial amendments were adopted at both markups. The subcommittee markup began with a complete substitute amendment by Chairman Kanjorski being adopted by voice vote. This substitute changed the NBCR provisions, delaying the make available provisions until 2009 and lowering the deductible to 3.5% with a 0.5% increase per year. It also included a requirement for biennial reporting on the TRIA program by the Treasury and changed the composition of the independent commission created by the bill to make recommendations on the program. Several amendments to reduce the 10 year extension of the program were rejected, as was one to require full recoupment of federal funds expended beyond the $27.5 billion aggregate retention amount in current law. Amendments adopted by the subcommittee included one by Representative Gary Ackerman to include the Secretary of Homeland Security in the certification of a terrorist attack under TRIA and one by Representative Richard Baker to apply the lower trigger amount in the retrospective reset provisions to the entire country rather than just to the affected area.

The full committee markup began with an amendment by Chairman Frank making a number of technical changes and three primary substantive changes. First, Chairman Frank's amendment changed the reset provisions, removing the retrospective reset altogether and applying the prospective reset provisions to the entire country. Thus, if there is a future terrorist attack resulting in more than $1 billion in damages, the trigger would by reduced to $5 million and the insurer deductible would be reduced to 5% for those insurers suffering terrorism losses. Second, it included temporary preemptions from state rate and form approval laws for NBCR coverage mandated under the bill. Third, it established a "terrorism buy down fund" in the U.S. Treasury which would essentially allow insurers to put aside reserves that would grow tax-free to cover losses from future terrorist attacks that are not reimbursed by TRIA. The U.S. Treasury could also borrow from this fund to cover the federal share of a future terrorist attack. The committee adopted a number of additional amendments, including (1) an exemption for small insurers from the requirement to make NBCR coverage available; (2) the return of farmowners multiple peril as a TRIA-covered line; (3) the specific allowance for insurers to partner in meeting the requirement to make NBCR coverage available; (4) the indexing of the various dollar amounts in the bill to an unspecified measure of inflation; (5) the provision for a report by the Secretary of the Treasury in the event that the Secretary decides not to recoup expended federal funds beyond $27.5 billion; (6) the extension of the program for 15 years, to the end of 2022; and (7) an increase in the post-reset deductible by 0.5% per year. The amended bill was forwarded to the full House by a vote of 49-20.

The Congressional Budget Office (CBO) issued a cost estimate for H.R. 2761 on September 6, 2007. CBO found that the bill as reported would increase direct spending by $3.7 billion from 2008 to 2012 and $10.4 billion from 2008 to 2017. This spending would be offset by additional revenues of about $100 million from 2008 to 2012 and $2.0 billion from 2008 to 2017. Since the cost estimate found that an increase in the budget deficit, or decrease in surplus, would result from the bill, it may run afoul of the "pay-as-you-go" (PAYGO) rule adopted by the House at the beginning of the 110th Congress.[18] In response to the PAYGO issues, the special rule (H.Res. 660) under which TRIREA was considered on the House floor included a self-executing amendment that inserted language into the underlying bill that would require passage by Congress of a joint resolution before any funds could be expended. H.Res. 660 provides for expedited consideration of this future resolution, including a waiver of all points of order against it and its consideration. This requirement for future congressional action introduces uncertainty to the TRIA program that did not exist before. It is unclear exactly how the insurance market might react to this uncertainty, should this language become law.

H.R. 2761 was brought up on the House floor under H.Res. 660 on September 19, 2007. The rule made in order two floor amendments and a motion to recommit with instructions.

The manager's amendment (H.Amdt. 801) by Chairman Frank changed the bill to include the NBCR deductible in the reset provisions, modified the certification process for an NBCR attack, indexed the dollar amounts in the bill specifically to the Consumer Price Index for All Urban Consumers (CPI-U), and made a variety of technical and conforming changes. It passed on the House floor 426-1. The other amendment (H.Amdt. 802) was offered by Representative Steve Pearce. It would have changed the increase in the deductible under the post-attack reset provisions from 0.5% per year to 1% per year. This amendment failed by a vote of 194-230. The motion to recommit with instructions was offered by Representative David Drier and failed by a vote of 196-228. The House then passed the bill as amended by a vote of 312-110. H.R. 2761 was received in the Senate on September 20, 2007, read twice, and referred to the Committee on Banking, Housing, and Urban Affairs.

To summarize, H.R. 2761 as passed by the House included provisions that would make the following changes to the current Terrorism Risk Insurance Program:

- Extend the TRIA program for 15 years, until the end of 2022.
- Make spending by the program contingent on passage of a future joint resolution.
- Add coverage for domestic terrorist acts in the program.
- Add the Secretary of Homeland Security to the certification process.
- Add group life insurance to the program with a separate set of retentions and deductibles.
- Return farmowners multiple peril as a covered line.
- Reduce the general trigger to $50 million.
- Require insurers to cover nuclear, biological, chemical, and radiological (NBCR) terrorist attacks starting in 2009.
- Lower insurer deductible for NBCR attacks to 3.5% immediately and then raise that number by 0.5% per year in the future.
- Increase the federal share of NBCR losses from 85% to as high as 100% for attacks causing over $100 billion in losses.
- Temporarily preempt state laws on rate and form filing for NBCR coverages.
- Provide the possibility of relief from NBCR requirement to smaller insurers.
- Reset individual insurer deductibles to 5% and the program trigger to $5 million in the aftermath of a future terrorist attack (or series of attacks) that causes more than $1 billion in damage. Deductible reset would be only for insurers who suffer losses.
- Increase the post-reset insurer deductibles by 0.5% per year.
- Establish a "Terrorism Buy-Down Fund" that would essentially allow insurers to put aside reserves that would grow tax-free to cover future losses that are not reimbursed by TRIA. The fund would also be available to the Secretary of the Treasury to cover the federal share of TRIA losses.
- Restrict life insurers' use of foreign travel as an underwriting tool.
- Index the dollar amounts in the program to future inflation.

The Office of Management and Budget released a Statement of Administration Policy[19] on H.R. 2761 that indicated "if H.R. 2761 as reported were presented to the President, his senior advisors would recommend that he veto the bill." The Administration indicated that it objected to the length of term of the extension, as well as the increase in the federal role and the expansion of the scope of coverage.

Terrorism Risk Insurance Program Reauthorization Act of 2007 (TRIPRA)

The Senate Banking, Housing, and Urban Affairs Committee marked up this original bill on October 17, 2007. While Senator Charles Schumer discussed possible amendments in the markup session, no amendments were voted on in committee. The bill was ordered reported to the full Senate on a vote of 20-1. Chairman Dodd introduced the bill, now numbered S. 2285, on November 1, 2007, and the committee report (S.Rept. 110-215) was issued the same day.

S. 2285 is a relatively straightforward reauthorization of the existing TRIA program. The two primary changes that it would make to the program are (1) extend it for seven years, until 2014; and (2) add coverage for domestic terrorist attacks to the program. In addition, it would modify slightly the annual liability cap, and require the Secretary of the Treasury to promulgate regulations on determining payments, should losses exceed $100 billion rather than leaving this determination to a future Congress. The bill would call for reports from the Government Accountability Office (GAO) on the possibility of insurance coverage for NCBR events (within one year) and on the affordability and availability of terrorism insurance in specific markets (within 180 days). In addition, the President's Working Group on Financial Markets would be tasked to continue its analysis of the longer term availability and affordability of terrorism risk insurance, and to report on this subject in 2010 and 2013.

CBO issued a cost estimate for TRIPRA on October 29, 2007. It found that the bill would increase direct spending by $3.1 billion from 2008 to 2012 and by $6.6 billion from 2008 to 2017. This spending would be offset by increased government receipts of $100 million from 2008 to 2012 and $1.5 billion from 2008 to 2017. No official Statement of Administration Policy has been released on the Senate bill. Treasury Secretary Paulson, however, has indicated in a letter that the Administration would be willing to accept the bill as it passed the committee.[20]

END NOTES

[1] L. James Valverde, Jr. and Robert P. Hartwig, "9/11 and Insurance: The Five Year Anniversary," available on the Insurance Information Institute website at [http://server.iii.org/yy_obj_data/binary/760752_1_0/September%2011%20Anniversary. pdf].

[2] Emmett J. Vaughan and Therese Vaughan, *Fundamentals of Risk and Insurance* (Hoboken, NJ: John Wiley & Sons, 2003), p. 41.

[3] P.L. 90-448, 82 Stat. 476. The act also created state "Fair Access to Insurance Requirements" (FAIR) plans and a Federal Crime Insurance Program.

[4] "Terror Insurance Drag on Real Estate Still Climbing," Real Estate Roundtable, September 19 2003, available at [http://www.rer.org/media/newsreleases/TRIA_Survey_15billion_Sept19_2002.cfm].

[5] "Moody's Downgrades Securities on Lack of Terrorism Insurance," *Wall Street Journal*, September 30, 2002, p. C14.

[6] "Office-Building Demand Rises Despite Vacancies," *Wall Street Journal*, July 24, 2002, p. B6.

[7] P.L. 107-297, 116 Stat. 2322. See CRS Report RS21444, *The Terrorism Risk Insurance Act of 2002: A Summary of Provisions*, by Baird Webel.

[8] See [http://www.treasury.gov/offices/domestic-finance/financial-institution/terrorism-insurance/] for the latest details. One exception was the study on availability that was to be done by August 2003. This has yet to be delivered to Congress.

[9] See [http://www.ustreas.gov/press/releases/js2618.htm].

[10] *Marketwatch: Terrorism Insurance 2006*, Marsh Inc., p. 7.

[11] Ibid., p. 8.

[12] Ibid., p. 9.

[13] *Property Terrorism Update: TRIA in the Balance*, Aon Inc., pp. 31-33.

[14] U.S. Department of Treasury, Report to Congress, *Assessment: The Terrorism Risk Insurance Act of 2002* (June 30, 2005), pp. 4, 64.

[15] *Marketwatch: Terrorism Insurance 2006*, Marsh Inc., p. 10.

[16] For additional information, see CRS Report RL33177, *Terrorism Risk Insurance Legislation in 2005: Issue Summary and Side-by-Side*, by Baird Webel.

[17] The full committee markup began on July 26, but H.R. 2761 was the last of a number of bills to be marked up.

[18] See CRS Report RL33850, *The House's "Pay-As-You-Go" (PAYGO) Rule in the 110th Congress: A Brief Overview*, by Robert Keith, for more information on PAYGO.

[19] See [http://www.whitehouse.gov/omb/legislative/sap/110-1/hr2761sap-r.pdf].

[20] Relevant text of this letter was provided to CRS by the Department of the Treasury. This was also reported in the press. See [http://www.politico.com/news/stories/1007/6394.html].

In: Terrorism Insurance
Editor: Miguel H. Palacios
ISBN: 978-1-60741-794-1

Chapter 3

TERRORISM INSURANCE: STATUS OF COVERAGE AVAILABILITY FOR ATTACKS INVOLVING NUCLEAR, BIOLOGICAL, CHEMICAL, OR RADIOLOGICAL WEAPONS

United States Government Accountability Office

WHY GAO DID THIS STUDY

The Terrorism Risk Insurance Act of 2002 (TRIA) is credited with stabilizing insurance markets after the September 11, 2001, attacks by requiring insurers to offer terrorism coverage to commercial property owners (property/casualty insurance), and specifying that the federal government is liable for a large share of related losses. While TRIA covers attacks involving conventional weapons, insurers may use exceptions that may exclude coverage for attacks with nuclear, biological, chemical, or radiological (NBCR) weapons, which has raised concerns about the potential economic consequences of such attacks. TRIA's 2007 reauthorization directed GAO to review (1) the extent to which insurers offer NBCR coverage, (2) factors that contribute to the willingness of insurers to provide NBCR coverage, and (3) policy options for expanding coverage for NBCR risks. To do this work, GAO reviewed studies and reports and interviewed more than 100 industry participants about the availability of NBCR coverage in the market.

GAO provided a draft of this chapter to the Department of the Treasury and the National Association of Insurance Commissioners (NAIC). Treasury and NAIC said that they found the report informative and useful. NAIC did express what it said was a philosophical difference of opinion with GAO's characterization of risk-based premiums for workers' compensation insurers.

WHAT GAO FOUND

Consistent with the findings of a September 2006 GAO report on the market for NBCR terrorism insurance, property/casualty insurers still generally seek to exclude such coverage from their commercial policies. In doing so, insurers rely on long-standing standard exclusions for nuclear and pollution risks, although such exclusions may be subject to challenges in court because they were not specifically drafted to address terrorist attacks. Commercial property/casualty policyholders, including companies that own high-value properties in large cities, generally reported that they could not obtain NBCR coverage. Unlike commercial property/casualty insurers, insurers in workers' compensation, group life, and health lines reported generally providing NBCR coverage because states generally do not allow them to exclude these risks.

Commercial property/casualty insurers generally remain unwilling to offer NBCR coverage because of uncertainties about the risk and the potential for catastrophic losses, according to industry participants. Insurers face challenges in reliably estimating the severity and frequency of NBCR attacks for several reasons, including accounting for the multitude of weapons and locations that could be involved (ranging from an anthrax attack on a single building to a nuclear explosion in a populated area) and the difficulty or perhaps impossibility of predicting terrorists' intentions. Without the capacity to reliably estimate the severity and frequency of NBCR attacks, which would be necessary to set appropriate premiums, insurers focus on determining worst-case scenarios (which with NBCR weapons can result in losses that would render insurers insolvent). For example, a nuclear detonation could destroy many insured properties throughout an entire metropolitan area. Workers' compensation, group life, and health insurers that generally cannot exclude NBCR coverage from their policies also face challenges in managing these risks. For example, workers' compensation insurers said they face challenges in setting premiums that they believe would cover the potential losses associated with an attack involving NBCR weapons.

GAO reviewed two proposals that have been made to address the lack of NBCR coverage in the commercial property/casualty market. The first proposal, part of an early version of the bill to reauthorize TRIA in 2007, would have required insurers to offer NBCR coverage, with the federal government assuming a greater share of potential losses than it would for conventional attacks. Some industry participants supported this proposal because insurers otherwise would not offer NBCR coverage and because a substantial federal backstop was necessary to mitigate the associated risks. However, others said that some insurers might withdraw from the market if mandated to offer NBCR coverage, even with a substantial federal backstop. In a second proposal by some industry participants, the federal government would assume all potential NBCR risks through a separate insurance program and charge premiums for doing so. However, critics said the government might face substantial losses on such an NBCR insurance program because it might not be able to determine or charge appropriate premiums.

December 12, 2008

The Honorable Christopher J. Dodd
Chairman
The Honorable Richard C. Shelby
Ranking Member Committee on Banking, Housing, and Urban Affairs
United States Senate

The Honorable Barney Frank
Chairman
The Honorable Spencer Bachus Ranking Member
Committee on Financial Services
House of Representatives

While the September 11, 2001, terrorist attacks killed nearly 3,000 people and resulted in an estimated $32.5 billion in insured losses as of 2006, analysts estimate that casualties and property damage involving unconventional weapons, such as nuclear, biological, chemical, or radiological (NBCR) materials, could be substantially worse under some scenarios.[1] For example, under a RAND Corporation simulation of a terrorist-detonated nuclear explosion in the Port of Long Beach, California, 60,000 people could die instantly, another 150,000 people could require emergency medical treatment, and losses could reach $1 trillion.[2]

Although the Terrorism Risk Insurance Act of 2002 (TRIA) requires companies that offer commercial property/casualty insurance (i.e., coverage for building damage and related legal costs for injuries to third parties) to provide coverage for terrorist attacks and specifies that the federal government assume a significant share of the associated financial responsibility, insurers' standard exemptions may exclude coverage for terrorist attacks involving NBCR materials.[3] While TRIA has been credited with stabilizing markets for terrorism insurance for conventional weapons, such as explosives, Members of Congress, academics, and policyholders have expressed concerns about a potential lack of coverage for terrorist attacks involving NBCR materials. In particular, they have stated that a substantial amount of uninsured losses could prolong economic recovery associated with an NBCR attack.

In a September 2006 report, we analyzed issues related to insurers' coverage for terrorist attacks involving NBCR weapons in commercial property/casualty policies as well as in other insurance lines, including workers' compensation, group life, and health.[4] We found that many commercial property/casualty insurers and reinsurers (companies that offer insurance to insurers) sought to exclude NBCR coverage from their policies or place significant restrictions on such coverage, largely because of potentially catastrophic losses associated with an NBCR attack. Although insurers reported that they would rely on standard policy exclusions for nuclear and pollution risks to generally limit exposure to NBCR risks, we noted that such exclusions may be challenged in courts.[5] We found that although insurers in other lines also were concerned about attacks involving NBCR materials, state regulators generally did not permit these insurers to exclude such risks from their policies. State workers' compensation laws generally require workers' compensation insurers to cover all risks, including claims from terrorist acts involving NBCR materials, and some state regulators do not allow life and health insurers to exclude such risks from their policies.

Unlike commercial property/casualty and workers' compensation insurers, life and health insurers would not be eligible for federal reimbursement for terrorism losses under TRIA.[6]

In December 2007, Congress passed and the President signed the Terrorism Risk Insurance Program Reauthorization Act of 2007, which extended the federal TRIA program until 2014.[7] The 2007 Reauthorization Act directed us to update our analysis of issues related to NBCR coverage. Specifically, the act required us to review (1) the extent to which insurers and reinsurers offer coverage for NBCR attacks; (2) the factors that contribute to the willingness of insurers and reinsurers to provide coverage for NBCR attacks and their ability to manage these risks; and (3) any public policy options for expanding coverage for these risks, given current insurance market conditions.

To address our objectives, we reviewed reports and studies on terrorism insurance for NBCR risks and interviewed more than 100 insurance industry participants about the availability of NBCR coverage in the market, factors contributing to the availability of NBCR coverage, and their views on options to expand the market for NBCR coverage. For coverage in commercial property/casualty and workers' compensation markets, we interviewed officials and representatives from state regulators, rating agencies, risk modeling firms, insurer and policyholder trade associations, national and regional insurance and reinsurance brokers, insurance and reinsurance companies, and policyholders in a variety of industries, in six geographic markets (Atlanta; Boston; Chicago; New York; San Francisco; and Washington, D.C.) that received different rankings for terrorism risk by an industry analyst. We interviewed some participants in specialized insurance markets, including a nuclear pool, Bermuda reinsurers, and a national broker with expertise in environmental insurance.[8] Furthermore, we interviewed private insurers that provide workers' compensation insurance and a judgmental sample of nine state workers' compensation funds that generally provide insurance for employers that cannot obtain it in the private market. Our analysis of NBCR coverage and capacity in the life and health insurance industries was more limited. We reviewed our September 2006 report and interviewed state insurance regulatory officials in California; Georgia; Illinois; Massachusetts; New York; and Washington, D.C., about NBCR coverage. We also interviewed representatives from several group life and health insurers with a large market share nationwide and in these same states. Although we selected industry participants to broadly represent national and specific market conditions, our sample may not represent the universe of insurers, insurance brokers, policyholders, and regulators. As a result, we could not generalize the results of our analysis to the entire national market for terrorism insurance for NBCR attacks in the commercial property/casualty, workers' compensation, life, and health insurance markets. To obtain views on the advantages and disadvantages of some public policy options for expanding coverage for NBCR risks, we reviewed options proposed in legislation, suggested by industry participants, or discussed in our prior reports or in other reports. See appendix I for more detailed information on our scope and methodology.

We conducted this performance audit from January 2008 to December 2008, in accordance with generally accepted government auditing standards. Those standards require that we plan and perform the audit to obtain sufficient, appropriate evidence to provide a reasonable basis for our findings and conclusions based on our audit objectives. We believe that the evidence obtained provides a reasonable basis for our findings and conclusions based on our audit objectives.

Results in Brief

Consistent with findings in our 2006 report, representatives of most commercial property/casualty insurers we contacted said that they continue to exclude coverage for terrorist attacks involving NBCR materials, and representatives from several reinsurance companies that do offer such coverage reported placing significant restrictions on it. Insurance representatives reported that they continued to rely on long-established exclusions, such as the nuclear and pollution exclusions, to exclude or limit coverage. However, some insurance industry participants said the applicability of these exclusions, particularly the pollution exclusion, could be challenged in court because the exclusions were not specifically developed to address terrorist attacks. In addition, representatives from policyholders, such as the owners of large properties in cities that are viewed as being at high risk of attack, including New York City and San Francisco, generally reported that they did not have coverage for attacks involving NBCR materials because (1) their insurers did not offer it; (2) they viewed available coverage as being too expensive to purchase (such as five times higher than their total property insurance costs); or (3) they had not sought coverage. Furthermore, due to the limited amount of NBCR coverage, some property owners said they had set up their own insurance companies, called captive insurers, specifically to cover the risks associated with such attacks.[9] Unlike commercial property/casualty insurance policies, workers' compensation, group life, and health insurance policies generally provide NBCR coverage because these insurers generally are not able to exclude such coverage. Workers' compensation insurers generally are required to cover losses resulting from injuries sustained at the workplace, and state regulators generally review the terms for offering such coverage, including price and policy limits. Representatives from life and health insurers also reported that state regulators generally have not permitted them to exclude NBCR risks from their policies, although representatives of an insurer and a state regulator we interviewed reported some exceptions that indicate some policies may exclude or limit coverage for NBCR risks.

Commercial property/casualty insurers and reinsurers generally do not offer or strictly limit NBCR coverage because of the uncertainties about the risk and the potential for catastrophic losses, according to industry participants, and insurers that are required to provide such coverage—in workers' compensation, life, and health—reported some challenges in managing the associated risks. Property/casualty insurance industry participants we contacted told us that NBCR risks generally are uninsurable because insurers lack a reliable means to estimate the severity (because of the wide range of potential weapons and targets) and frequency (because of the impossibility of predicting terrorists' intentions) of such attacks.[10] Without the ability to reliably estimate the severity and frequency of NBCR attacks, insurers lack a basis for setting premium rates to compensate for their potential losses. As a result, industry representatives reported that insurers and reinsurers focus on the most catastrophic NBCR attacks, under scenarios with widespread financial damage. For example, some representatives of property/casualty insurers told us that the scale of a nuclear blast could affect a far greater portion of an insurer's portfolio than a truck bomb of conventional explosives, potentially rendering insurers that chose to offer NBCR coverage insolvent. Although representatives of workers' compensation insurers in the private market told us they may not offer coverage to employers in geographic areas considered to be at higher risk of terrorist attack, representatives from state funds—state-established insurers generally designed to accept all employees—reported that they generally are required to cover all employers, regardless of location or risk level.[11] Both private workers' compensation insurers and state funds we contacted also said that they face challenges in managing NBCR risks, such as setting premiums that they believe would cover the potential losses associated with a terrorist attack that involved NBCR weapons (workers' compensation insurers in many states are permitted to add a uniform surcharge of one penny per $100 of employee payroll to cover terrorism risks, including those involving NBCR materials). While group life and health insurers may have somewhat more regulatory flexibility than certain workers' compensation insurers to manage NBCR risks, they may face challenges in doing so. For example, group life insurers, due to competitive pressure within the industry, may be unwilling to restrict coverage in certain geographic markets perceived to be at higher risk of terrorist attack. Furthermore, partly due to their limited experience with the effects of attacks involving NBCR materials, representatives from group life and health insurers said it is difficult for them to develop risk-based premiums to cover potential losses from an NBCR attack.

The two proposals that we identified and reviewed to increase the availability of insurance coverage for terrorist attacks involving NBCR materials focus on the commercial property/casualty market because such coverage is largely unavailable in that market and would involve the federal government assuming most or all of the associated financial risks.[12] One recent legislative proposal would amend TRIA to mandate that insurers make NBCR coverage available and would provide greater federal financial support for attacks involving NBCR weapons compared with the current TRIA program for terrorism attacks in general.[13] A variety of industry participants supported this proposal. For example, representatives of one insurer said that, given insurers' reluctance to cover terrorist attacks involving NBCR materials, the only way to make such coverage available would be to mandate that commercial property/casualty insurers offer NBCR coverage. To offset the potential costs to insurers in providing such coverage, the federal government would assume a greater share of the potential losses. A recent RAND study also concluded that requiring insurers to cover NBCR risks may reduce potential taxpayer costs in comparison to the current situation in which the federal government may be asked to cover a large share of uninsured losses from an NBCR attack, as it has done after natural catastrophes and terrorist attacks.[14] However, other industry participants said that even with a reduced exposure to the costs of an NBCR attack, some insurers might withdraw entirely from the commercial property/casualty insurance market if they were required to offer coverage for attacks involving NBCR materials. Under a separate proposal suggested by some industry participants, the federal government would assume complete financial liability for policyholders that elect coverage and charge premiums for doing so. Insurers would be responsible for administering the program similar to other federal insurance programs such as the National Flood Insurance Program. While some industry participants said that the only way to help ensure the availability of NBCR coverage would be for the federal government to assume all of the potential costs, others disagreed for several reasons. For example, some expressed concerns about the potential costs of such a program. The federal government may face substantial challenges in establishing appropriate premiums for NBCR risks and, therefore, could face significant losses, which has been the case in other federal insurance programs. In addition, some said insurance companies may not have the experience needed to provide claims adjustors and other personnel for areas affected by attacks involving NBCR materials.

We provided a draft of this chapter to the Department of the Treasury (Treasury) and the National Association of Insurance Commissioners (NAIC) for their review and comment.[15] In oral comments, Treasury officials said that they found the report informative and useful. They also provided technical comments that we incorporated where appropriate. NAIC provided written comments that are reprinted in appendix II. In these comments, NAIC officials said they found our report useful and informative and agreed with its analysis of the various policy options, but also said that they had a philosophical difference of opinion with some statements in our draft report. In particular, NAIC commented on our discussion on the ability of workers' compensation insurers to charge risk-based premiums to employers perceived as being at higher risk for terrorist attacks. NAIC said that the draft report implied that state insurance regulators, due to voter and legislative pressure, keep premium rates artificially low for workers' compensation insurers rather than relying on actuarial science. NAIC disputed what they characterized as our implied contention and suggested that the recent profitability of the workers' compensation insurance industry indicates that premiums have not been suppressed by regulatory actions. We made clarifications to the draft to address certain NAIC comments. For example, we more fully described the surcharges that workers' compensation insurers may levy for covering losses from terrorist attacks, including those involving NBCR weapons. However, the draft report in no way meant to imply that state insurance regulators succumb to voter and legislative pressures in approving rates, and simply reported that workers' compensation insurers and some regulators we contacted for both our September 2006 report and this chapter said that they did not believe the permissible surcharge would be sufficient to cover the potential losses associated with an NBCR attack.[16] Given that NBCR risks may not fully satisfy the principles of insurability (as we said in our September 2006 report), statements by representatives of workers' compensation insurers that question whether the permitted surcharge would be sufficient to cover potential losses do not appear to be inherently unreasonable. We also note that while NAIC reports that workers' compensation insurers have been profitable over the past several years, this does not mean that any premiums collected from this surcharge would be sufficient to cover the losses associated with a future NBCR attack. NAIC also provided technical comments that we incorporated as appropriate. We also obtained technical comments from several state insurance regulators and other organizations on a draft of this chapter, which were incorporated as appropriate.

Background

Congress enacted and the President signed TRIA in 2002 to help restore confidence and stability in commercial property insurance markets after private insurers withdrew terrorism coverage in the wake of the September 11 attacks. TRIA requires that commercial property/casualty insurers, including (among others) workers' compensation insurers, "make available" coverage for certified terrorist events under the same terms and conditions as other, nonterrorism coverage. Following a terrorist attack, the federal government would reimburse insurers for 85 percent of their losses after insurers pay a deductible of 20 percent of the value of each company's prior year's direct earned premiums.[17] Federal reimbursement is activated when aggregated industry losses exceed $100 million and is capped at an annual amount of $100 billion.[18] TRIA also would cover losses caused by NBCR terrorist attacks if the insurer had included this coverage in the insurance policy.

Originally enacted as a 3-year program, TRIA was reauthorized in 2005; in 2007, Congress extended the program until 2014. In the deliberations over the 2005 and 2007 Reauthorization Acts, Congress considered mandating that commercial property/casualty insurers offer coverage for NBCR risks, with significantly lower deductibles and copayments.[19] Congress also considered adding group life insurance to the TRIA program, so that group life insurers could receive reimbursements for the majority of their claims from terrorist events, including NBCR attacks.[20] Members of Congress supporting this provision argued that group life insurers were vulnerable to the same extraordinary losses from a terrorist attack as other insurance lines and could become insolvent after a catastrophic event. However, Treasury testified that the Administration did not want to expand TRIA to cover group life insurers, citing some reports that the group life insurance market has remained competitive after September 11. The NBCR requirement and the group life provisions were not included in the final TRIA reauthorizing legislation.

Variation in Potential Weapons involving NBCR Materials and Examples of Prior Attacks

Government and other experts have stated that terrorist attacks involving NBCR weapons could affect people and property in a variety of ways, depending on the weapon used as well as the location of the attack. Table 1 provides examples of attacks using NBCR weapons as well as some of their potential effects.

Previous attacks involving NBCR materials in United States and Japan also illustrate a range of consequences. In September and October 2001, contaminated letters laced with anthrax were sent through the mail to two U.S. senators and members of the media. As a result, 22 individuals contracted anthrax disease, and 5 of these individuals died. In 1984, the Rajneeshee religious cult in Oregon contaminated salad bars in local restaurants with salmonella bacteria to prevent people from voting in a local election. Although no one died, 751 people were diagnosed with the food-borne illness. In 1995, 12 people were killed and many more were injured after Aum Shinrikyo, a State Department-designated terrorist organization, released the chemical nerve agent Sarin in the Tokyo subway.

Overview of State Regulation of Insurance and Workers' Compensation Insurance Providers

States have the primary responsibility for regulating the insurance industry in the United States, and the degree of oversight varies by insurance line and state. In some lines of insurance, state regulators guide the extent of coverage by approving the wording of policies, including the explicit exclusion of some perils. Regulators coordinate their activities, in part, through NAIC. According to an NAIC representative, while practices vary by state, state regulators generally review prices for personal lines of insurance and workers' compensation policies but not for commercial property/casualty policies. In most cases, state insurance regulators perform neither rate nor form review for large commercial property/casualty insurance contracts because it is presumed that businesses have a better understanding of insurance contracts and pricing than the average personal-lines consumer. Reinsurers generally are not required to obtain state regulatory approval for the terms of coverage or the prices they charge.

Table 1. Types of Potential NBCR Attacks and Their Effects

Threat	Type of threat	Example of an event	Potential effects
Nuclear	Detonated device	A 10-kiloton nuclear device is detonated in a large city	Destruction of buildings with subsequent high-energy radiation and extreme heat forming a cloud from which highly lethal radioactive material would fall.
Biological	Anthrax	A concealed device sprays anthrax spores in a city	Agents—such as anthrax and smallpox—can multiply in the human body, signifi-cantly increasing their effects. Many bio-logical agents are highly virulent and toxic; they may have an incubation period so that their effects are not seen for hours to days.
Chemical	Nerve agent	Sarin is sprayed into the ventilation system of three commercial buildings in a city	Because many chemicals are inherently hazardous, the release of chemicals or the risk of contamination at chemical facilities poses a potential threat to public health and the economy. Approximately 800,000 shipments of hazardous materials such as liquid chlorine and ammonia travel daily throughout the United States by ground, rail, air, water, and pipeline. Many of these mate-rials are explosive, flammable, toxic, and corrosive and can be extremely dangerous when improperly released, and a release could cause injury or death and significant environmental damage.
Radiological	Dispersal device	"Dirty bombs" are detonated in three cities in regional proximity	A dirty bomb uses conventional explosives to disperse radioactive material across the immediate area. The primary short-term exposure hazard to humans would be in-halation of radioactive material suspended in the dust and smoke from the explosion, leading to radiation injury and potential death.

Source: GAO.

Note: For additional information on NBCR attacks, see GAO, *Homeland Security: First Responders' Ability to Detect and Model Hazardous Releases in Urban Areas Is Significantly Limited*, GAO-08-180 (Washington, D.C.: June 27, 2008); *Combating Nuclear Terrorism: Federal Efforts to Respond to Nuclear and Radiological Threats and to Protect Key Emergency Response Facilities Could Be Strengthened*, GAO-08-285T (Washington, D.C.: Nov. 15, 2007); *Chemical and Biological Defense: Updated Intelligence, Clear Guidance, and Consistent Priorities Needed to Guide Investments in Collective Protection*, GAO-07-113 (Washington, D.C.: Jan. 19, 2007); and *Combating Terrorism: Need for Comprehensive Threat and Risk Assessments of Chemical and Biological Attacks*, GAO/NSIAD-99-163 (Washington, D.C.: Sept. 14, 1999).

Because state laws generally require employers to carry workers' compensation insurance, which covers employees for death or injuries as a result of a workplace incident, employers generally obtain coverage either from a private insurance company or from a fund established by the state.[21] Twenty-six states have established separate funds, either run by the state or as a separate company, according to the American Association of State Compensation

Insurance Funds (AASCIF), and most of these states provide workers' compensation coverage for all employers seeking it. An NAIC official told us that when state governments began requiring employers to purchase workers' compensation coverage, many states established separate funds to provide a mechanism to ensure coverage for those employers that could not obtain it in the private market. The majority of state funds are competitive, meaning that the state fund competes for business with other private insurers. However, in four states, the state fund is the sole insurer for workers' compensation, unless an employer is permitted to self-insure.[22] The National Academy of Social Insurance reported that in 2006, just over half of workers' compensation benefits (50.38 percent) were paid by private insurers, with just under half coming from state funds (19.66 percent), federal programs (5.98 percent), and self-insured employers (23.98 percent).[23]

Most Commercial Property/Casualty Insurers and Reinsurers We Contacted Exclude or Limit Coverage for NBCR Risks, While Workers' Compensation, Life, and Health Insurers Generally are Required to Offer Such Coverage

Commercial property/casualty insurers and reinsurers generally seek to exclude coverage for NBCR risks or place significant restrictions on such coverage. According to industry participants, insurers interpret the language of longstanding exclusions developed for nuclear and pollution risks as excluding terrorist attacks involving NBCR weapons, but the use of such exclusions may be challenged in court. Representatives from policyholders from a variety of industries, including real estate, financial services, and hospitality, also told us that they do not have NBCR coverage either because a very limited amount of NBCR insurance is available or they do not view the rates for available coverage as reasonable. A few policyholders also reported self-insuring these risks through captive insurers. Representatives from workers' compensation, life, and health insurers we contacted generally reported that they cover losses from terrorist attacks, including those involving NBCR materials, because they said state regulators generally do not allow these insurers to exclude such risks.

NBCR Coverage Generally is Unavailable in Commercial Property/Casualty Insurance and Reinsurance Policies, but the Exclusions Used to Limit Coverage could be Challenged in Court

While few market surveys that we identified specifically have addressed the availability of property/casualty insurance for terrorist attacks involving NBCR materials, our interviews with a range of industry participants suggests that such coverage continues to be limited.[24] Representatives from the majority of the insurers and reinsurers we interviewed said that their companies generally do not offer NBCR coverage or offer a limited amount of such coverage. Representatives of large insurance and reinsurance trade associations, as well as national insurance brokers, also reported a general lack of coverage for NBCR risks. According to a representative from a large national insurance broker, he was not aware of any primary insurers that offered NBCR coverage as part of their standard property/casualty policies. The representative said that some insurers that offer "stand-alone" terrorism insurance policies offer NBCR coverage, but demand for this product is minimal due to its relatively high price and restrictions. Although representatives of several reinsurers based in Bermuda told us that their companies offer some NBCR coverage, the reported restrictions on these policies help illustrate some of the limitations of the available coverage. For example, the policy language of one reinsurance contract we reviewed limited NBCR coverage only to losses resulting from the initial "force or violence" of the NBCR terrorist attack and did not cover long-term effects, such as resulting illnesses or business interruption.

Insurance companies seek to limit their coverage for NBCR risks by relying on long-standing exclusions for nuclear and pollution risks, which already have been approved by state regulators. As we stated in our September 2006 report, insurers have written exclusions related to nuclear hazard risks into their standard policies for decades, generally to protect themselves from losses related to nuclear power accidents. Furthermore, representatives from the Insurance Services Office (ISO), a national organization for the property/casualty insurance industry that develops standardized policy language designed to comply with regulatory requirements, said that insurers also typically exclude coverage for losses caused by pollution and contamination. ISO representatives told us that the pollution exclusion was developed to exclude coverage for the release of many different substances—such as asbestos or pesticides—that could cause harm to people and the environment. Some insurance representatives said that the pollution exclusion could be applied to biological and chemical agents released in a terrorist attack.

Because these exclusions were developed for other purposes, some regulators and insurance industry participants said that their use by insurers in the event of an attack involving NBCR materials could be challenged. Representatives from one large insurer told us that language in the nuclear hazard exclusion may not be clear enough to apply to a nuclear terrorist attack. Similarly, representatives from a large insurance company said the pollution exclusion would not apply unless the terrorist attack itself was deemed to be a polluting event. An official from the New York Insurance Department also said that the Department did not interpret the definition of "pollutants" in the standard pollution exclusion forms to apply to biological and chemical terrorist attacks. Courts determine whether a particular substance is or is not a pollutant based upon, among other things, the language in the policy, the facts and circumstances of the case, and the law of jurisdiction.[25] As we stated in our September 2006 report, given the potential for litigation and court interpretation, insurers and other industry experts have raised some concerns as to how effectively the pollution exclusion would protect insurers against losses resulting from an NBCR terrorist attack.

Property/casualty insurers also may face potential exposure to losses from NBCR attacks as the result of state requirements, but it is difficult to assess the extent of this exposure. According to industry officials, 16 states—including California, Illinois, and New York—require property/casualty insurers to cover losses from fire following an event, regardless of the cause of fire.[26] As we reported in 2006, in the case of a nuclear bomb detonation, once the property was destroyed, insurers could dispute the extent to which fire (covered in "fire following" states) or the blast (excluded by the nuclear exclusion) caused the damage. However, given the potential devastation resulting from a nuclear terrorist attack—including potentially widespread destruction and protracted evacuations—it may be difficult for insurers, policyholders, regulators, and courts to resolve any issues related to the cause of loss.

Property/Casualty Policyholders Report That NBCR Coverage Generally is Unavailable or Available at Prices They View as Unaffordable

Information we obtained from commercial policyholders in a range of industries across the country also indicate that property/casualty coverage for NBCR risks is very limited. For example, we interviewed representatives from real estate companies that own large, high-value commercial properties (such as office buildings or hotels) in cities—including Chicago, New York, and San Francisco—that generally are viewed as being at high risk of terrorist attack. While representatives from these companies said that they generally were able to obtain coverage for terrorist attacks that involve conventional weapons, such as truck bombs, they generally did not have NBCR coverage. In addition, results from a recent survey of risk managers conducted by the Risk and Insurance Management Society, Inc. (RIMS), show that commercial policyholders generally have not been offered NBCR coverage in their insurance policies. Although the RIMS survey has several limitations, it found that less than 15 percent of the respondents had coverage for NBCR attacks.[27] Furthermore, representatives we contacted from industries such as transportation, hospitality, entertainment and utilities also reported that they did not have NBCR coverage, or had limited coverage, such as for only chemical risks.[28]

Policyholders we contacted said that they generally lacked NBCR coverage because (1) their insurers did not offer it; (2) the prices quoted on the coverage that was available were viewed as too expensive to purchase; or (3) they did not seek coverage. For example, a representative of a shopping center development company with retail locations in various cities throughout the United States said that the company is concerned about the risks of NBCR attack and has sought insurance coverage. However, the representative said that the company has not been able to identify any insurers that would offer the company NBCR coverage or provide pricing information. In addition, representatives of a commercial real estate developer in Washington, D.C., said that quoted insurance premiums for NBCR coverage were five times higher than their total property insurance costs. Insurance brokers we contacted told us that although some of their commercial policyholder clients have inquired about NBCR coverage, the demand for such coverage is less than that for conventional terrorism coverage. As we stated in 2006, demand for conventional terrorism coverage is high in the commercial real estate sector because mortgage lenders generally require companies to purchase coverage. However, according to brokers and a lender that we interviewed, lenders do not require companies to secure coverage for NBCR terrorist attacks because such coverage is largely unavailable.

Due to concerns about the potential for NBCR attacks and the general lack of coverage offered by insurers, some policyholders said that they had established captive insurers to self-insure the risk and obtain federal reinsurance under TRIA.[29] Captive insurers are generally established by major corporations, such as large real estate companies, to self-insure a variety of risks. Corporations may create captives for several reasons, including to obtain coverage for certain risks that may no longer be provided by the private market (such as medical malpractice insurance), access additional coverage directly from a reinsurer, or reduce tax payments. According to a representative from an insurance broker that helps companies in establishing and managing captives, companies either may add NBCR coverage to an existing captive insurer or may create one to cover NBCR risks. For example, a representative from a national real estate company told us that he had difficulty finding terrorism insurance at prices viewed as reasonable and without restrictions, so the company established a captive that covered NBCR risks. Although captives may help some companies limit their potential exposure from NBCR attacks, available information suggests that captives are not widely used for this purpose, perhaps because companies may lack the financial resources necessary to do so.[30] To illustrate, representatives from 18 percent of the 39 policyholders we contacted and 6 percent of the 377 respondents to the RIMS survey that we have previously discussed reported using captives to insure NBCR risks.

Workers' Compensation, Life, and Health Insurers Generally Cover NBCR Risks Due to State Requirements

Unlike property/casualty insurers, workers' compensation insurers we contacted said that they offer NBCR coverage because they generally are not permitted to exclude it under state laws and regulations. As we found in 2006, applicable state laws generally require workers' compensation insurers to cover all perils, including those from NBCR risks. Under state workers' compensation laws, employers are responsible for covering unlimited medical costs and a portion of lost earnings for injuries or illnesses that occur during the course of employment, regardless of the cause, according to NAIC.

Similarly, we were told that group life insurers generally do not exclude NBCR coverage from their policies, according to regulators and industry participants. Officials from five of the six state insurance regulators that we interviewed reported that they do not allow terrorism or NBCR attacks to be excluded from life insurance policies.[31] However, officials from these regulatory agencies also said that their states had not enacted laws that explicitly require insurers to offer such coverage. Given the lack of statutory requirements, officials from Washington, D.C., told us that group life insurers in the District could exclude NBCR risks from their coverage. However, representatives from the American Council of Life Insurers, a national trade association for life insurers, reported that they were not aware of the use of NBCR exclusions and believed that group life insurers generally cover NBCR risks; officials from several large life insurance companies confirmed that they provided coverage.

Finally, health insurers also generally cover NBCR risks, according to state regulators, representatives from America's Health Insurance Plans, and health insurers we contacted. According to industry participants, health insurers generally are required to pay claims, regardless of the cause that led to the claim. Insurance regulatory officials from several states with locations viewed as high risk—California, Georgia, Illinois, Massachusetts, and New York—told us that they do not permit health insurers to exclude NBCR coverage from their policies. However, regulatory officials in Washington, D.C., said that health insurers were not mandated to cover NBCR risks in the District and insurers had filed policies with NBCR exclusions. In addition, a representative from one large health insurer said that the insurer would invoke the *force majeure* clause—a general contract provision used to relieve parties from their responsibilities due to circumstances beyond their control, such as acts of God—to exclude NBCR risks. However, representatives from two state regulators we interviewed told us they were not familiar with the *force majeure* clause, and an official from the Georgia Department of Insurance told us he did not think the clause would apply to terrorist acts involving NBCR materials.

POTENTIAL FINANCIAL CONSEQUENCES OF NBCR ATTACKS LIMIT PROPERTY/CASUALTY INSURERS' WILLINGNESS TO OFFER COVERAGE; INSURERS FOR OTHER LINES OF INSURANCE REPORT LIMITED CAPACITY TO MANAGE ASSOCIATED RISKS

Commercial property/casualty insurers and reinsurers generally are not willing to provide coverage for NBCR attacks or place significant restrictions on the coverage they offer because of the uncertainties surrounding such attacks and their potential for generating catastrophic losses. Although private workers' compensation insurers generally have greater flexibility than state funds to limit their exposure to losses from NBCR attacks by not offering coverage to certain employers, both private insurers and state funds may face other challenges in managing the risks associated with terrorist attacks involving NBCR weapons, such as limits on their ability to price such risks and obtain private reinsurance. Life and health insurers may also face challenges in managing NBCR risks, such as competitive market pressures and challenges in establishing appropriate premiums for their potential exposures.

Commercial Property/Casualty Insurers and Reinsurers Are Concerned about the Uncertainty and Potential Enormity of Losses from NBCR Attacks

As we stated in our September 2006 report, many insurers view terrorist attacks, particularly attacks involving NBCR materials, as an uninsurable risk because of uncertainties about the severity and frequency of such attacks. Insurance companies typically manage and assess risk on the basis of their expected losses, using historical information about the range of damages (severity) and the number of incidents in a given period of time (frequency). For some risks, such as those related to driving automobiles, insurers have access to a substantial amount of statistical and historical data on accidents, from which they can predict expected losses and then calculate premiums that are adequate to cover these losses. Large claims from automobile accidents also generally do not occur to a large number of policyholders at the same time, which serves to limit insurers' exposures. In contrast, catastrophes, including natural disasters such as hurricanes as well as terrorist attacks, present unique challenges to insurers because they may result in substantial losses and are relatively infrequent. To address these challenges, insurers may use computer models developed internally and by outside firms to help estimate the financial consequences of various disaster scenarios, and in some cases, to develop appropriate premiums. However, as we have previously noted, due to data limitations, estimating the potential consequences of terrorist attacks is fundamentally different and substantially more difficult than forecasting natural catastrophes. For example, substantial data are available on the frequency and severity of hurricanes, but the United States has experienced relatively few terrorist attacks, particularly those involving NBCR materials.[32]

Attack in New York City			Estimated losses (dollars in billions)	Estimated fatalitie s (numbers in thousands)
Type	Form	Size		
Chemical	Sarin gas	1,000 kg ground dispersal	$34	6,000
Radiological	Dirty bomb	15,000 curies of Cesium-137	43	A few
Biological	Anthrax	1 kilogram anthrax slurry	118	34,000
		10 kilogram anthrax slurry	254	80,000
		75 kilogram anthrax slurry	501	207,000
Nuclear	Nuclear power plant sabotage	Nearby nuclear powerplant	217	A few
	Nuclear bomb	Battlefield 1 kiloton	205	1,300,000
		Tactical 5 kiloton	584	3,000,000

Figure 1. Examples of Potential Property/Casualty and Workers' Compensation Losses from Different NBCR Scenarios in New York City

Sources: Risk Management Solutions, Inc.; Art Explosion (images).

Note: According to Risk Management Solutions, Inc, the dirty bomb scenario would use a TNT detonation to disperse spent fuel rods of Cesium-137. In the anthrax slurry attack, anthrax would be aerosolized and released in a watery mixture by a high pressure hose. A battlefield 1 kiloton bomb would come from a suitcase-size bomb, and the tactical 5 kiloton bomb would come from a larger nuclear device.

Estimates of the potential severity of attacks involving NBCR materials may be particularly difficult to produce for several reasons, according to insurance industry participants and representatives from firms that have developed computer models for catastrophe risks. For example, as we previously have discussed, a wide range of potential weapons are associated with NBCR attacks, which could result in varying amounts of property damage as well as injuries and deaths (see fig. 1). While estimates for the damage resulting from nuclear blast in an urban area exceed the loss estimates for a chemical attack on a single building or facility, loss estimates also may vary for different types of attacks using the same agent. For example, one modeling firm has produced a scenario in which a moving truck releases anthrax in a highly populated urban area creating total insured losses of $144 million, 20 times higher than if the anthrax were released through a sprayer inside the ground floor of a large building.[33] Representatives of insurers and reinsurers we interviewed expressed concerns about models' ability to account for all of the potential losses associated with an NBCR attack, such as business interruption and litigation costs, which may be difficult to quantify. In addition, a recent report by one modeling firm stated that decisions about the extent of cleanup required for nuclear and radiological contamination likely will be made after the attack, creating further uncertainties about the cost of rebuilding or remediation.[34]

Insurers also face challenges with developing frequency estimates for NBCR attack scenarios. Representatives of risk modeling firms told us they use worldwide incidents of

NBCR attacks and researchers' opinions on terrorists' capabilities and potential targets to develop estimates for NBCR event frequency. However, some insurance industry participants described frequency estimates of NBCR attacks as too subjective to be used as a basis for pricing coverage, because views on the frequency of attacks vary. For example, while one modeling firm stated in a recent report that its estimates for the frequency of terrorist attacks are 0.6 events per year, or 2.0 events every 3 years, the representative of a large commercial property/casualty insurer said that his firm viewed the risk as occurring once every 8 years.[35] Furthermore, insurance experts said that terrorists continue to adjust their strategies, thereby making past attacks a poor predictor of future events.

Because insurers and reinsurers face challenges in reliably estimating the severity and frequency of terrorist attacks involving NBCR materials and setting appropriate premiums, industry representatives reported that their companies focus on the most catastrophic attacks under scenarios with widespread financial losses. For example, some representatives of property/casualty insurers told us that the scale of a nuclear blast could have a devastating impact on an insurer that chose to offer NBCR coverage, because such an attack could destroy or render uninhabitable many or all buildings within a large metropolitan area. In contrast, we have previously reported that since TRIA was enacted, insurers have some ability to limit their potential losses from terrorist attacks involving conventional weapons such as truck bombs, because the damage resulting from such attacks might be confined to a smaller geographic area, such as a radius of several blocks from the attack.[36] Representatives of insurers we contacted told us their companies may limit their property/casualty coverage in locations viewed as at high risk for a terrorist attack, such as New York City; however, they reported that the potential losses from an NBCR attack could far exceed what their company would be able to cover. As we reported in 2006, academic experts and industry participants have pointed out that insurers have little incentive to insure catastrophic events that might jeopardize their financial soundness and solvency, so insurers remain unwilling to offer coverage for NBCR attacks.

Private Workers' Compensation Insurers Have Somewhat Greater Flexibility to Manage NBCR Risks by Choosing Which Employers to Offer Coverage, but Private Insurers and State Funds Face Other Risk Management Challenges

Although private and state workers' compensation insurers generally must cover losses resulting from NBCR attacks, private companies generally have greater flexibility in managing their exposures to losses from NBCR attacks under the TRIA program. Specifically, private insurers may choose to which employers they will offer coverage.[37] Accordingly, representatives of private insurers reported that their companies have monitored or limited coverage offerings to employers with employees concentrated in locations considered to be at higher risk for an NBCR attack. For example, representatives of smaller, more regionally based insurers said their companies decided not to offer coverage for certain employers that have employees concentrated in densely populated locations, or limited their overall coverage offerings for workers' compensation in urban areas.[38]

In contrast to private insurers, state workers' compensation funds generally are unable to limit their NBCR risks on the basis of employers' perceived risk levels. State laws and regulations generally require state funds to provide coverage to all employers—regardless of their location or risk level—and serve either as the state's sole insurer or as the insurer of last resort. While officials from some state funds we contacted said that they were concerned about exposure to losses from an NBCR attack, they also said the nature of their funds' operations might limit that exposure to some degree. For example, representatives from some funds said that because they offered coverage to a significantly large group of employers of varying sizes across the state, their exposure to losses from NBCR attacks was somewhat diversified.

Finally, representatives of private workers' compensation insurers and state funds told us that they faced some challenges in managing NBCR exposures, such as pricing the risk and obtaining adequate amounts of private reinsurance. Recognizing workers' compensation insurers' exposure to terrorism risks, state regulators in at least 37 states, including the District of Columbia, have permitted insurers to apply a statewide surcharge, or additional premium, (which is on average about 1 cent per $100 payroll) to cover the potential losses from terrorist attacks, including those involving NBCR materials.[39] The National Council on Compensation Insurance, Inc. (NCCI), developed statewide surcharges based on the results of a model, as a way for insurers that underwrite in states that belong to NCCI to cover potential losses from terrorism, including those using NBCR materials.[40] NCCI officials told us that their surcharges generally are uniform across a state and insurers using this surcharge generally cannot levy higher surcharges for employers they perceive to be at higher risk of terrorist attack. Furthermore, NCCI's surcharges were developed to cover potential losses from terrorist attacks involving conventional as well as NBCR weapons. Officials from the New York Compensation Rating Board, which develops workers' compensation rate proposals for the state of New York (which does not belong to NCCI), also told us the state's surcharges were developed to cover potential losses from both conventional and NBCR terrorist attacks. However, as we stated in our 2006 report, state regulators and insurance representatives advised us that any surcharges that insurers may be permitted to charge for NBCR exposure likely would not cover potential losses. Similarly, representatives of private workers' compensation insurers we contacted for this chapter that underwrite coverage in locations considered at high risk for terrorist attacks said that their surcharges for terrorism may not cover all of their potential exposure. In addition, representatives of many of the private insurers and some of the state funds we interviewed said that they had little to no private reinsurance for NBCR risks, and that they would rely on TRIA in the event of a catastrophic NBCR attack.

Group Life and Health Insurers May Face Challenges in Managing NBCR Risks

In contrast to workers' compensation insurers, life and health insurers may have somewhat more flexibility to manage the risks associated with terrorist attacks involving NBCR materials. For example, unlike workers' compensation insurers, the prices charged by group life insurers generally are not subject to state regulatory approval. Group health insurers generally are able to negotiate the terms of health care coverage with employers and employees, unlike workers' compensation benefits that are state-mandated.

However, based on the limited amount of work we conducted, we found that for terrorist attacks involving NBCR materials, group life and health insurers face the following risk-management challenges:

- Group life insurers may not actively seek to limit the amount of coverage that they offer in geographic markets perceived to be at high risk of attack, according to representatives from the American Council on Life Insurance (ACLI) and several large companies we contacted. According to these officials, the group life insurance market is highly competitive, with insurers competing to cover employers, even in densely populated urban areas at risk for terrorist attacks. Furthermore, life insurers' use of models to manage the risks associated with providing coverage in densely populated areas may be limited. We spoke with representatives from two group life insurers that reported that while they have started to use models to review the impact of catastrophic scenarios, they lack specific data on the location of employees from some employers to monitor their concentration of insured individuals. An ACLI representative said that group life insurers with exposures across the country may be better able to manage risks from an NBCR attack than smaller, more regional insurers with portfolio concentrations near target locations.
- We also previously reported on the difficulties group life insurers face in charging higher premium rates to employers perceived to be at higher risk of terrorist attacks, including attacks involving NBCR materials.[41] Life insurers price their products on the basis of mortality tables derived from experience with prior insurance contracts and calibrated to the effects of individual characteristics, such as smoking, or group characteristics, such as occupation type. According to ACLI, group life insurance policies currently are not designed or priced to account for catastrophic financial losses and mass casualties from an unpredictable terrorist attack with an NBCR weapon.
- Similarly, health insurers may face difficulties in setting premium rates to address the risks of terrorist attacks, including those involving NBCR materials. For example, health insurers said that they generally price coverage on the basis of previous experience with insured populations, and that without knowing the frequency and severity of NBCR risks, they could not develop actuarially sound prices for such a risk. Furthermore, because illnesses or symptoms of illnesses resulting from NBCR attacks could take years to develop, it might be very difficult for insurers to establish appropriate premiums for such long-term risks.

Proposals to Increase Coverage for NBCR Attacks in the Property/Casualty Market Have Advantages and Disadvantages

Because the current commercial property/casualty market generally lacks coverage for terrorist attacks involving NBCR materials, the two proposals we reviewed to increase the availability of such coverage focus on that market. The proposals involve the federal government assuming most or all of the associated financial liabilities of such attacks. For example, an early version of the bill to reauthorize TRIA in 2007 would have required insurers to make NBCR coverage available and would have lowered their exposure to potential losses. While such a proposal may increase the availability of NBCR insurance, some industry participants believe it would disrupt insurance markets. Alternatively, some industry participants have suggested that the federal government should fully insure losses from terrorist attacks involving NBCR materials, similar to other federal disaster insurance programs. This program could help ensure the availability of NBCR insurance, according to some industry participants, but others said the program could result in substantial losses to the federal government.

Proposal 1: Amend TRIA to Require Insurers to Make NBCR Coverage Available with the Federal Government Assuming Greater Financial Responsibility for Potential Losses

The House of Representatives initially passed an early version of the 2007 reauthorization of TRIA that would have amended the act to (1) require insurers to make NBCR coverage available to policyholders, and (2) require the federal government to assume a relatively high proportion of the associated financial risk. With certain exceptions, the proposal would have required insurers to offer coverage for NBCR attacks under terms, amounts, and other coverage limitations that did not differ materially from their coverage for other types of risks. The proposal would have allowed an insurer to exclude NBCR coverage altogether (except for workers' compensation or other state coverage requirements) or offer a separate NBCR terrorism policy at different terms, amounts, and other coverage limitations than other types of coverage, if a policyholder rejected an insurer's initial offer for coverage. To compensate insurers for the risks associated with providing NBCR coverage, the proposal initially would have set insurers' TRIA deductibles for such attacks at 3.5 percent of direct earned premiums, substantially lower than the 20.0 percent deductible insurers would pay under the current program for terrorist attacks in general.[42] In addition, under this proposal, insurers' copayment, or additional share of losses, for an NBCR attack would have varied depending on the size of the losses associated with the attack. In the case of a smaller NBCR attack, an insurer would have paid 15 percent of its losses after paying its deductible, and for very large NBCR attacks, 5 percent.[43] Additionally, the proposal would have permitted insurers to voluntarily reserve some of their conventional and NBCR terrorism premiums, tax-free, in a fund maintained by Treasury to cover the TRIA deductibles or copayments associated with losses from future terrorist attacks.[44]

Given insurers' general reluctance to provide NBCR coverage, some industry participants we contacted stated that this proposal was reasonable. For example, a representative from one insurer said that unless mandated to do so, insurers would not offer coverage for NBCR risks. Representatives from other insurers and industry participants, including regulators, told us that limiting insurer losses for NBCR events would help insurers better manage risks associated with NBCR attacks. With their financial exposures limited, insurers could more easily develop terms and conditions for NBCR coverage to policyholders and offer the coverage at lower rates. In addition, some industry participants said that the provision in the legislation allowing for separate pricing of NBCR coverage would (1) allow insurers to tailor insurance coverage and prices to the type of terrorist attack, and (2) provide policyholders with the choice of purchasing NBCR and conventional terrorism coverage together or separately.

A recent study by the RAND Corporation found that requiring insurers to offer NBCR coverage, with the federal government assuming significant financial liability for the associated losses from large attacks could be beneficial.[45] For example, the RAND study stated that under such a program the number of policyholders purchasing coverage would increase substantially from current levels.[46] Furthermore, the study concluded that the federal government's expected outlays for compensation and assistance following attacks involving NBCR materials actually might decrease. Given that property/casualty coverage for NBCR attacks is largely unavailable, in the event of such an attack, the study noted that the federal government might decide to provide a large amount of disaster assistance or other compensation following an attack, as it has done for the victims of natural catastrophes and terrorist attacks. If insurers were required to provide some coverage for NBCR attacks, the study concluded that the federal government's expected costs could be somewhat lower under certain conditions than otherwise would be the case.[47]

Some industry participants also suggested that insurers could use different strategies in addition to TRIA to further manage the risks associated with providing NBCR coverage, as would be mandated under this proposal. In particular, some participants said they favored insurers forming risk pools or changing tax laws to permit insurers to set aside tax-deductible reserves to offset some of the losses associated with terrorist (including NBCR) attacks, similar to provisions in the legislative proposal.[48] We have reported that establishing a group of insurance companies to pool their assets could allow insurers to provide a greater amount of coverage for the entire market than could be provided by each individual company. Furthermore, as we discussed in our prior reports, allowing either a pool or individual insurers to maintain tax-deductible reserves could provide the industry with incentives to expand capacity to cover catastrophic risks, such as attacks with NBCR materials.[49] Table 2 provides information on existing or proposed pooling arrangements in the United Kingdom and the United States that are designed to help insurers manage the risks associated with terrorist attacks involving NBCR materials or accidents involving nuclear materials.

However, other industry participants cautioned that requiring insurers to provide NBCR coverage, even with the federal government assuming a relatively high percentage of the associated financial exposure, could have adverse consequences for insurance markets. For example, a variety of industry participants said that under such a mandate, insurers may be less willing to offer property/casualty coverage and may withdraw from the market or not offer coverage in areas viewed as at high risk of attack. Some industry participants expressed particular concern about the impact that such a proposal would have on smaller insurers. While this proposal substantially would have lowered the deductible for attacks involving NBCR materials, a few industry participants said that the proposed copayments for such attacks still could be substantial for smaller insurers. The officials said that smaller insurers may lack the financial capacity to cover such potential costs.

Table 2. Examples of Proposed or Existing Pooling Arrangements

Pooling arrangement	Program description	Program funding	Reserves taxed?
Pool Reinsurance Company, Limited (Pool Re)	A mutual reinsurer in the United Kingdom that provides reinsurance for terrorism and NBCR risks for members' commercial property policies. Terrorism coverage is optional for policyholders, and parti-cipation is voluntary for insurers, but member insurers must reinsure all terrorism coverage with Pool Re.	In the event of an act of terr-orism, coverage from Pool Re takes effect after members pay individual deductibles. If the resources of Pool Re are exhausted, the United Kingdom government provides an unlimited guarantee. Pool Re pays the government a premium for this guarantee and would have to repay the Treasury any amount received from the guarantee.	No
Industry proposed U.S. reinsurance pool	A national reinsurance pool for commercial property terr-orism risk, including NBCR risks. Insurers would continue to charge policyholders their own rates for terrorism cover-age and would purchase rein-surance from the pool.	In the event of a terrorist attack, the insurance industry would pay 5 percent of losses, and the pool would pay 95 percent of losses up to $40 billion. If the pool did not have the resources to pay its share of losses, it could issue bonds. The federal govern-ment would be responsible for losses in excess of $40 billion, up to $100 billion. Losses above $100 billion would be reviewed by Congress.	No
Price Anderson reinsurance pool	Provides for liability coverage for all commercial nuclear reactors in the event of a catastrophic incident. Approximately 22 insurance companies participate in American Nuclear Insurers (ANI), a joint underwriting association that underwrites and administers the policies. Insurers participate on a voluntary basis, subject to certain membership requirements.	All reactors are required to carry $300 million in primary liability insurance, which is written primarily by ANI. ANI's premium reserve fund and capacity from member insurers cover claims on these policies. If losses exceed the primary coverage, a pool financed by retrospective premiums equally assessed to all commercial nuclear reactors provides reinsurance. A 5 percent surcharge per commercial nuclear reactor may be imposed to provide additional funding to cover damages resulting from a nuclear incident.	According to ANI, member insurers only pay taxes on portion of premiums they receive as reimbursement for their expenses.

Sources: GAO, Aon, and ANI.

Note: For more information on Pool Re, see GAO, *Terrorism Insurance: Alternative Programs for Protecting Insurance Consumers,* GAO-02-175T (Washington, D.C.: Oct. 24, 2001). Aon, which is a global insurance broker, issued a report on the commercial property terrorism market that included a long-term pooling proposal to address the issue of terrorism risk in the United States. See Aon, *Property Terrorism Update, TRIA in the Balance* (New York, N.Y.: October 2005).

In addition, some industry participants and policyholders said that this proposal could be prohibitively costly to policyholders and taxpayers. As we have previously discussed, industry participants said that estimates of the severity and frequency of terrorist attacks involve many uncertainties, making pricing difficult. Consequently, some industry participants said that insurers, faced with a mandate of providing NBCR coverage, might set premiums at rates they consider necessary to compensate for the risks of a catastrophic attack, which could deter many commercial entities from purchasing such coverage. For example, two researchers we contacted said that when Pool Re expanded its coverage to include NBCR risks after the September 11 attacks, prices for terrorism coverage doubled. In addition, some industry participants said that if the federal government were liable for a greater portion of insured losses resulting from an NBCR attack, then the overall costs to the taxpayer from that attack could be significant. Furthermore, although the RAND study concluded that costs to the federal government could be reduced by requiring insurers to offer NBCR coverage, the study noted that in the case of extremely large NBCR attacks, the federal government's financial liability could be larger than if it did not participate in the market for terrorism insurance and require insurers to offer NBCR coverage. We also note that the federal government's total costs could be higher under this option than the current situation where NBCR coverage is generally unavailable, and Congress later decided to provide additional funding to pay for uninsured losses from such an attack.

Finally, information from our previous work, as well as interviews with some industry participants, raises questions about whether establishing pools or permitting insurers to maintain tax-deductible reserves materially would enhance available coverage for terrorist attacks, including those involving NBCR materials.[50] According to industry participants and a study by a global consulting firm on a proposed pool for workers' compensation coverage for terrorism risk, a reinsurance pool might not create new industry capacity or bring in additional capital to support writing more business.[51] The study noted that if the overall industry does not have enough capital to manage the risk of an NBCR attack, then neither would an industry pool that simply combines existing industry capital in a new structure. Furthermore, we have reported that overall insurance capacity might not increase if a pool or individual insurers were allowed to establish tax-deductible reserves. Because reinsurance premiums already are tax-deductible, insurers would receive similar tax benefits from traditional reinsurance, pool reinsurance, or individual reserves.

Therefore, insurers might substitute the pool reinsurance or individual reserves for their current reinsurance program, if that program includes coverage for NBCR attacks.[52]

Proposal 2: Federal Government Completely Insures Losses for Terrorist Attacks involving NBCR Materials, with Insurers Administering the Program

Given concerns about the potential financial and other consequences of requiring insurers to provide NBCR coverage, some industry participants we contacted suggested that the federal government should develop a separate program to insure against such attacks. Under this proposal, the federal government would serve as insurer, covering all losses for NBCR attacks and charging premiums for providing these services. The insurance industry's role largely would be administrative, as some industry representatives reported that the industry would have the staff, processes, and experience in place to manage such tasks. For example, insurance companies could be responsible for collecting premiums, adjusting claims, and disbursing claims payments from the government to policyholders. This proposal could be similar to other federal insurance programs shown in table 3, where the government assumes most, if not all, of the risk.[53] These other programs generally were created because of gaps in coverage in the private market or the perception that the risks were uninsurable.

While some industry analysts said that this proposal was the only way to ensure that NBCR coverage would be widely available, others expressed concerns about the potential costs of such a program to the federal government and its effects on the private market. With the government responsible for most, if not all, of the losses in the event of a terrorist attack involving NBCR materials, several industry participants expressed concerns about the potentially large post-disaster costs for the federal government and, ultimately, taxpayers. We note that other government disaster insurance programs have proven to be costly and have administrative challenges. For example, we have reported that while NFIP and the Federal Crop Insurance Program were created to provide affordable insurance coverage, they do not collect enough in premiums to fund potential losses from catastrophic disasters. Therefore, Congress has had to appropriate funds after disasters, such as floods, to pay catastrophic claims.[54] Given the difficulties associated with reliably estimating the potential severity and frequency of terrorist attacks involving NBCR materials as discussed in this chapter, the federal government may face substantial challenges in establishing premiums sufficient to offset the risks involved in providing insurance coverage for such attacks.

Table 3. Examples of Current and Past Federal Insurance Programs

Program name	Program description	Insurance industry role
Federal Crop Insurance Corporation	Insurance for farmers in the event their crops are damaged by floods, droughts, or other national disasters. The Federal Crop Insurance Corporation offers farmers varying subsidy rates for crop insurance, depending on the level of protect-tion they seek.	Private insurance companies sell and service crop insurance policies. Insurance companies share a perc-entage of the risk of loss or oppor-tunity for gain associated with each insurance policy written.Companies also receive a percentage of the pre-mium on policies sold to cover their administrative costs.
National Flood Insurance Program (NFIP)	Residential and commercial insur-ance available to participating co-mmunities to cover losses due to flooding. Policyholders may pay a subsidized, discount-ed, or full-risk rate premium, depending on the lo-cation of the property, amount of coverage, and when the community joined the program.	Private-sector insurance agents and adjusters sell, service, and adjust claims. Participating insurance companies receive an expense allowance for their services and are required to remit premium income in excess of this allowance to the NFIP Fund. The companies also receive a fee for adjusting and settling claims.
FAA Aviation Insurance Program	Prior to September 11, this program provided coverage for international flights into hostile territories. The program has since extended cover-age to domestic flights, as an alter-native to commercial third-party war risk insurance.	None. FAA issues policies, collects applicable premiums, and pays claims.
War Damage Corporation	A government-owned corporation that provided insurance against loss or damages from enemy attack during World War II. It was formed as the War Insurance Corporation on December 13, 1942, after the attack on Pearl Harbor. All policies expired in 1947, and the War Dam-age Corporation was terminated, except for purposes of liquidation.	The government hired insurers as agents and reimbursed them for their expenses. According to a Treasury official, they assumed risk for 10 percent of losses in excess of net premiums collected, subject to an industry cap.

Sources: GAO, the Coalition to Insurance against Terrorism, and Treasury.

In addition to the large potential costs to taxpayers, industry participants expressed other concerns about the federal government assuming complete financial responsibility for potential NBCR property/casualty losses. For example, some industry participants, including regulators, did not think that the government should be responsible for all of the potential losses from an NBCR attack and that insurers could assume some of the risk. Furthermore, we have previously reported that some industry participants believe that too much federal government involvement in disaster relief crowds out private insurance and reduces the private market's ability and willingness to provide insurance-based solutions to covering catastrophe risk.[55] Finally, while insurers would play a largely administrative role under this proposal, some insurers expressed reservations about this potential responsibility because they have no experience training, equipping, and sending claims adjusters and other personnel into areas where NBCR materials have been released.

AGENCY COMMENTS AND OUR EVALUATION

We provided a draft of this chapter to the Department of the Treasury and NAIC for their review and comment. In their oral comments, Treasury officials said that they found the report informative and useful. They also provided technical comments that were incorporated where appropriate.

NAIC provided written comments on a draft of this chapter, which have been reprinted in appendix II. In their comments, NAIC stated that the report was materially accurate and they agreed with our discussion on proposed policy proposals for expanding NBCR coverage in the commercial property/casualty market. However, NAIC reported a philosophical difference of opinion with comments in the draft report about the ability of workers' compensation insurers to charge risk-based premiums for attacks involving NBCR weapons. NAIC stated that our draft report contained references that implied that state insurance regulators, due to voter and legislative pressure, keep premium rates artificially low for workers' compensation insurers rather than relying on actuarial science. NAIC disputed what it characterized as our implied contention and suggested that the recent profitability of the insurance industry indicates that premiums have not been suppressed by regulatory actions.

We made clarifications in the draft to address certain NAIC comments, such as more fully describing the surcharges that workers' compensation insurers may levy for covering losses from terrorist attacks, including those involving NBCR weapons. However, the draft report in no way meant to imply that state insurance regulators succumb to voter and legislative pressures in approving rates, and simply reported that workers' compensation insurers and some regulators we contacted for both our September 2006 report and this chapter said that they did not believe the permissible surcharges would be sufficient to cover the potential losses associated with an NBCR attack.[56] Given that NBCR risks may not fully satisfy the principles of insurability, as we said in our September 2006 report, statements by representatives of workers' compensation insurers that question whether the permitted surcharges are sufficient to cover potential losses do not appear inherently unreasonable. As discussed in the final report, the permitted surcharge in many states is the same for conventional terrorist attacks and for those involving NBCR weapons and insurers generally are not permitted to levy higher surcharges for employers they perceive to be at higher risk of attack. Furthermore, we note that while NAIC reports that workers' compensation insurers have been profitable over the past several years, this does not mean that any premiums collected from this surcharge would be sufficient to cover the losses associated with a future NBCR attack.

NAIC also commented on statements in the draft report regarding the ability of group life insurers to manage exposures to NBCR risks. Specifically, NAIC said that the competitive nature of group life insurance markets has more of an impact on group life insurers' decisions to provide NBCR coverage in their policies than any regulatory constraints. NAIC stated that if one group life insurer were to exclude coverage for NBCR risks, and other group life insurers did not exclude such coverage, the insurer excluding NBCR risks would be at a competitive disadvantage. NAIC concluded that employers may choose not to purchase coverage from the group life insurer that excluded NBCR risks, unless the price difference was substantial. We generally agree with NAIC that competitive market pressures may affect group life insurers' willingness to limit NBCR coverage, and note that the argument was included in the draft provided to NAIC for its review and comment. Nevertheless, we made some adjustments to the text to ensure that this analysis was better communicated throughout the final report. NAIC also provided additional technical comments and observations that were incorporated as appropriate.

We also sent excerpts of our draft report to the six state regulators discussed in this chapter (California, Georgia, Illinois, Massachusetts, New York, and Washington, D.C.) for their review. Three state regulators responded that they did not have any changes to our characterization of NBCR requirements in their states, and one regulator provided a technical comment that we made. We also provided excerpts of the draft report to five other organizations referenced in this chapter, and all five responded, some with technical comments that were incorporated where appropriate.

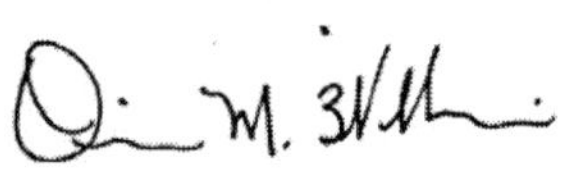

Orice M. Williams
Director, Financial Markets and
Community Investment

Appendix I: Objectives, Scope, and Methodology

Our objectives were to review (1) the extent to which insurers and reinsurers offer coverage for nuclear, biological, chemical, and radiological (NBCR) attacks; (2) the factors that contribute to the willingness of insurers and reinsurers to provide coverage for NBCR attacks and their ability to manage these risks; and (3) any public policy options for expanding coverage for these risks, given current insurance market conditions.

To address the first objective, we reviewed relevant studies and interviewed representatives of more then 100 organizations, including insurer and policyholder trade associations; individual policyholders; national insurance and reinsurance brokers; and insurance and reinsurance companies with knowledge of the commercial property/casualty, workers' compensation, group life, and health insurance markets nationwide and with expertise in specific geographic markets. We also interviewed local brokers, insurance companies, and local property owners in cities and regions with locations considered to be at high, moderate, and low risk of exposure to terrorist attacks. These locations included Atlanta; Boston; Chicago; New York; San Francisco; and Washington, D.C. We selected these markets on the basis of rankings of locations by risk of terrorism exposure from the Insurance Services Office (ISO), an insurance industry analytics firm. Insurers may use these rankings, which account for cities' risk of terrorist attacks and the potential for associated losses, as a basis for charging additional premiums for terrorism exposure, according to ISO and several regulators we contacted. We interviewed some participants in specialized insurance markets, including a nuclear pool, Bermuda reinsurers, and a national broker with expertise in environmental insurance. We spoke with representatives of policyholders that own hundreds of properties and other entities nationwide. These entities included large office towers in major U.S. cities, properties in proximity to high-profile federal buildings, hotels, industrial buildings, hospitals, sports stadiums, a chemical company, a railroad company, and residential properties in locations throughout the United States. In addition to one-on-one interviews, we also conducted group discussions with representatives of 14 policyholders at the annual Risk and Insurance Management Society, Inc. (RIMS), conference in San Diego, California, in April 2008. Although we selected industry participants to provide broad representation of market conditions geographically and by industry, their responses may not be representative of the universe of insurers, insurance brokers, policyholders, and regulators. As a result, we could not generalize the results of our analysis to the entire national market for commercial property/casualty, workers' compensation, group life, and health insurance. We determined that the selection of these sites and participants was appropriate for our objectives, and that this selection would allow coverage of locations considered to be at high, moderate, and low risk of exposure to terrorist attacks, and would obtain information related to NBCR coverage for major insurers, policyholders, and other organizations to generate valid and reliable evidence to support our work.

We also reviewed the Department of the Treasury's *2005 Report to Congress, Assessment: The Terrorism Risk Insurance Act of 2002* and its results from a survey of commercial property/casualty insurers on the coverage they offered for NBCR risks. We were limited in our ability to use this information because it was unclear from the survey question whether an insurer offered NBCR coverage in one commercial property/casualty policy or in all policies. We also reviewed results from a survey of risk managers conducted by RIMS of their membership. However, we also were limited in our ability to use results from this survey on purchase rates of NBCR insurance as a signal for approximating overall demand because of the low response rate (approximately 10 percent) to the survey.

To address the second objective, we selected large, national insurance companies to interview on the basis of their market share in the states we studied—California, Georgia, Illinois, Massachusetts, and New York as well as Washington, D.C. In the commercial property/casualty and workers' compensation market, these national insurance companies held from 37 to 52 percent of the market share in the states we studied, according to information provided by the Insurance Information Institute. In addition, we interviewed representatives of regional insurance companies in our selected markets. We also spoke with representatives of seven reinsurance companies, including two of the largest worldwide reinsurance companies as well as risk modeling firms, state regulators, and two credit rating agencies.

To select state workers' compensation funds, we compiled and analyzed available data on workers' compensation state funds based on information from the American Association of State Compensation Insurance Funds and the National Council on Compensation Insurance, Inc. We selected nine workers' compensation state funds on the basis of the

- presence of a metropolitan city in the state;
- presence of cities considered at risk for terrorist attacks, developed using estimates from ISO; and
- type of state fund—either monopolistic (fund is the sole insurer in the state) or competitive (fund competes with private insurers to offer workers' compensation coverage)—and its size.

To learn more about the coverage in the group life and health insurance markets and factors affecting that coverage, we interviewed state regulators in California; Georgia; Illinois; Massachusetts; New York; and Washington, D.C., as well as officials from the American Council of Life Insurers and America's Health Insurance Plans—two large national trade associations. We also interviewed several group life and health insurers with large shares of the market both nationally and in the selected states, as well as one large group life reinsurance company and a representative from a national brokerage firm with expertise in the reinsurance market for group life carriers. Although we selected insurers from each of the lines we studied to provide a broad representation of size and geographic scope, we could not generalize the results of our analysis to the entire population of private insurers or workers' compensation state funds.

To address the third objective, we reviewed options proposed in legislation, discussed in our prior reports or in other reports, or suggested by industry participants. We also interviewed academics, representatives from research organizations, and consumer interest groups. Although these discussions did not produce a consensus about what measures would increase the availability of NBCR coverage, for this chapter we focused on two proposals deemed viable by a variety of industry participants. We selected the proposal to amend Terrorism Risk Insurance Act to require insurers to make NBCR coverage available and lower insurers' deductibles and co-payments from a recent legislative proposal. We selected the option for the federal government to insure losses for terrorist attacks involving NBCR materials from interviews conducted with industry participants. We compiled and analyzed the views of the industry participants listed above on these two proposals and reviewed our prior reports to obtain information about other federal insurance programs. We did not attempt to evaluate the prospective impact of these proposals and, therefore, did not come to any conclusions about the advisability of implementing them.

We conducted this audit in Atlanta; Boston; Chicago; New York; San Diego; San Francisco; and Washington, D.C., from January 2008 to December 2008, in accordance with generally accepted government auditing standards. Those standards require that we plan and perform the audit to obtain sufficient, appropriate evidence to provide a reasonable basis for our findings and conclusions based on our audit objectives. We believe that the evidence obtained provides basis for our findings and conclusions based on our audit objectives.

Appendix II: Comments from the National Association of Insurance Commissioners

NAIC

National Association of Insurance Commissioners

November 18, 2008

Orice M. Williams, Director
Financial Markets and Community Investment
United States Government Accountability Office
441 G St. NW, Room 2440B
Washington, DC 20548

RE: GAO Report on Terrorism Insurance
Status of Coverage Availability for Attacks
Involving Nuclear, Biological, Chemical,
or Radiological Weapons

Dear Ms. Williams:

The National Association of Insurance Commissioners (NAIC) appreciates the opportunity to comment on the captioned GAO report. The NAIC is always pleased to work with the GAO to make sure that members of Congress and the public are informed about important regulatory and public policy matters.

The NAIC is a voluntary organization of the chief insurance regulatory officials of the 50 states, the District of Columbia and five U.S. territories. The NAIC's overriding objective is to assist state insurance regulators in protecting consumers and helping maintain the financial stability of the insurance industry by offering financial, actuarial, legal, computer, research, market conduct and economic expertise. Formed in 1871, the NAIC is the oldest association of state officials. For more than 135 years, state-based insurance supervision has served the needs of consumers, industry and the business of insurance at-large by ensuring hands-on, frontline protection for consumers, while providing insurers the uniform platforms and coordinated systems they need to compete effectively in an ever-changing marketplace.

There are some areas where the NAIC believes there are technical corrections needed and a few areas where there is a philosophical difference of opinion about what the GAO has concluded. Our suggested changes follow:

- The last sentence of the second paragraph of the Highlights says, "For example, state regulators generally do not permit workers' compensation insurers to charge risk-based premiums to employers." This is an area where the NAIC has a fundamental disagreement with the GAO's conclusion. The NAIC does not dispute that on occasion, regulators do not permit insurers to charge all that they wish. However, this reference and others imply that state insurance regulators are subject to voter and legislative pressure to keep premiums affordable and coverage readily available and succumb to these pressures instead of relying on actuarial science. The GAO seems to have fallen into a common trap of assuming that insurers and their actuaries have perfect information about what workers' compensation and terrorism losses will occur during the next

EXECUTIVE HEADQUARTERS	2301 McGee Street, Suite 800	Kansas City, MO 64108-2662	p | 816 842 3600	f | 816 783 8175
GOVERNMENT RELATIONS	444 N. Capitol Street, NW, Suite 701	Washington, DC 20001-1509	p | 202 471 3990	f | 202 471 3972
SECURITIES VALUATION OFFICE	48 Wall Street, 6th Floor	New York, NY 10005-2906	p | 212 398 9000	f | 212 382 4207

www.naic.org

APPENDIX II. (Continued)

year and how the economy will behave. The basic assumption made by the GAO and by academics that have concluded there is rate suppression, is that the actuaries working for insurers are always correct in their projections of the needed price for the future experience period and regulatory actuaries are always wrong if they disagree with the company actuaries. The truth arguably is somewhere in between. Projected loss costs to cover the insurer's exposure to losses vary widely depending on which risk modeling firm the insurer selects to produce its terrorism loss costs. If an insurer selects the output of a modeling firm that produces higher rates, the regulator might object and suggest that another modeling firm might be more appropriate. Your text and the work of academics that study this topic would brand that regulator as a rate suppressor, even if the insurer's future results prove that the regulatory actuary was correct. Recent financial performance for workers' compensation insurers shows that the industry is profitable with a 61.3% loss ratio for 2007, 60.7% for 2006 and 65.5% for 2005. Over the three year time span, property and casualty insurers were able to increase their policyholder surplus from $427 billion to $530 billion. If the regulators are actively engaged in rate suppression and not letting insurers charge risk-based prices, how are they able to operate so profitably?

- On page 2 of the report, the last sentence on the page says, "State insurance laws generally require workers' compensation insurers to cover all risks…" We suggest that you change "insurance" to "workers' compensation" as it is the workers' compensation laws not the insurance laws that contain this requirement.

- The industry opinion disputed in the first bullet point of the letter appears again on page 6 in the 15th through 18th lines. It is correctly attributed to industry participants, but is incorrect as most states have allowed workers' compensation insurers to add a charge for covering acts of terrorism. The industry might believe that the additional rate is not sufficient; however, it is incorrect to say they are not generally allowed to charge higher premiums.

- On page 6, lines 18 through 23 discuss the perspective of life insurers with regard to providing coverage for acts of terrorism on group life insurance contracts. We agree with the statements made, however, there is a missing element that is not captured in the text. It is generally the market conditions of the employee benefits market that have a greater influence on the coverages offered by group life insurers than any regulatory constraints. If one group life insurer decided it would not offer coverage for acts of terrorism, including NBCR, while other group life insurers offered the coverage, the one insurer excluding the coverage would be at a competitive disadvantage. Employers generally do not want to have to tell the surviving spouse and children that there is no compensation forthcoming for the loss of their loved one. Thus, the employer would have a natural tendency to select from the insurers providing the coverage rather than from those excluding the coverage, unless the price difference was substantial.

- On page 12, we offer updated numbers for your consideration to replace those included from the Insurance Information Institute. We would suggest the following amended sentence: The ~~Insurance Information Institute~~ National Academy of Social Insurance reported that in ~~2005~~2006, just over half of workers' compensation benefits (~~50.8~~50.38 percent) were paid by private insurers, with the other half coming from state funds (~~19.4~~19.66 percent), federal programs (~~5.9~~5.98 percent), and self-insured employers (~~23.8~~23.98 percent). We believe that NASI is the source for the numbers used by the Insurance Information Institute.

APPENDIX II. (Continued)

- On page 13, line 5 through 8, there is discussion about why workers' compensation insurers are not allowed to exclude coverage for acts of terrorism. The report says that it is "...because state regulators generally do not allow them to exclude such risks." A more accurate statement would be that state workers' compensation laws require the insurer to assume all of the obligations that an employer has to its employees as a result of work related accidents and injuries regardless of cause of loss. Further the mention for life insurers and health insurers misses the mark. See the comments for page 6, lines 18 through 23 above.

- On page 18, the last sentence in the second paragraph has further discussion on life insurance and coverage exclusions. The comments for page 6, lines 18 through 23 above also apply in this instance.

- On page 19, lines 1 through 8 discuss the *force majeure* clause and the possibility that health insurers would use the standard clause to relieve them of responsibility for providing coverage for acts of terrorism. We would generally agree with the official from the Georgia Department of Insurance who suggested that the *force majeure* clause probably would not apply to terrorists acts involving NBCR materials. The *force majeure* clause is generally found in contracts other than insurance and is intended to relieve one of the parties of performance demanded by the contract for unforeseen events beyond the control of the party. These would include natural disasters or other "Acts of God," war, riots, crimes or the failure of third parties—such as suppliers and subcontractors—to perform their obligations to the contracting party. *Force majeure* clauses are intended to excuse a party only if the failure to perform could not be avoided by the exercise of due care by that party. Taken to the extreme suggested by the industry representative, the *force majeure* clause could be used by homeowners insurers to deny claims for wind damage from a hurricane, damage from a riot or fire damage from a lightening strike (an Act of God). Clearly these contracts are intended to provide coverage for the very acts that the *force majeure* clause intends to disallow.

- On page 19, the sixth line of the paragraph in the middle of the page suggests that private insurers can "restrict coverage" to certain employers. The choice of language implies something that insurers cannot do—namely restrict coverage within an individual contract. What the private insurer can do is not offer any workers' compensation coverage to the employer. This paragraph also contains the disputed allegation that state regulators will not let insurers charge risk-based premiums. Please see the discussion in the first bullet point of this letter.

- On page 24, the last line of the first paragraph has a missing word that changes the meaning of the last sentence. We suggest you add "offerings" between "coverage" and "for." Without the additional word, the sentence could be read to say that the insurers somehow limited workers' compensation coverage, perhaps by adding a terrorism exclusion or other type of impermissible coverage limitation. With the addition of "offerings," it is clear that the insurer is limiting coverage by not offering to insure certain employers.

- On page 25, the allegation that regulators do not allow insurers to charge risk-based premiums appears again. Please refer to the explanation contained in the first bullet point of this letter.

- On page 25, the first paragraph mentions that the rate for terrorism insurance is the same throughout the state. It might be tradition, more than regulation; that is to blame for this circumstance. The NCCI and other state-based workers' compensation advisory organizations have not, to our knowledge, ever encouraged the use of territorial rating for workers'

APPENDIX II. (Continued)

compensation insurance. Workers' compensation is class rated using various occupational classifications that price the relative likelihood of the employees in the class to experience a work-related injury or illness. It is also experience rated where an employer's loss experience is compared to the expected average loss experience of all employers with similar employees and the individual employer's rate is adjusted either upward or downward based on whether its loss experience is better or worse than average expected loss experience.

- There is a discussion of the group life and health insurance challenges in managing NBCR risks that starts on page 25 and continues through page 27. The last bullet point in the section (page 26 and 27) has a discussion about how the insurer might have difficulty pricing NBCR risks because illnesses could take many years to develop. We do not disagree with the discussion; however, it seems to be missing one possible outcome. That is for the business to change health insurance providers. Thus the health insurer that was at-risk when the NBCR event occurred might not be the health insurer that ends up with the claim. The claim would instead go to the health insurer at-risk at the time the illness manifests itself.

Overall, the reviewers believed that the report was materially accurate with the exceptions noted in this letter. The reviewers agree with the discussion regarding the options presented in the report for Congress to consider.

Thanks again for all your hard work in making government accountable to the public that it serves.

Sincerely,

Andrew J. Beal,
Acting Executive Vice President and CEO

Related GAO Products

Terrorism Insurance: Status of Efforts by Policyholders to Obtain Coverage. GAO-08-1057. Washington, D.C.: September 15, 2008.

Terrorism Insurance Availability: Initial Results on Availability of Terrorism Insurance in Specific Geographic Markets. GAO-08-919R. Washington, D.C.: July 11, 2008.

Homeland Security: First Responders' Ability to Detect and Model Hazardous Releases in Urban Areas Is Significantly Limited, GAO-08-180. Washington, D.C.: June 27, 2008.

Natural Disasters: Public Policy Options for Changing the Federal Role in Natural Catastrophe Insurance. GAO-08-7. Washington, D.C.: November 26, 2007.

Terrorism Insurance: Measuring and Predicting Losses from Unconventional Weapons is Difficult, But Some Industry Exposure Exists. GAO-06-1081. Washington, D.C.: September 25, 2006.

Catastrophe Risk: U.S. and European Approaches to Insure Natural Catastrophe and Terrorism Risks. GAO-05-199. Washington, D.C.: February 28, 2005.

Terrorism Insurance: Effects of the Terrorism Risk Insurance Act of 2002. GAO-04-806T. Washington, D.C.: May 18, 2004.

Terrorism Insurance: Effects of the Terrorism Risk Insurance Act of 2002. GAO-04-720T. Washington, D.C.: April 28, 2004.

Terrorism Insurance: Implementation of the Terrorism Risk Insurance Act of 2002. GAO-04-307. Washington, D.C.: April 23, 2004.

Catastrophe Insurance Risks: Status of Efforts to Securitize Natural Catastrophe and Terrorism Risk. GAO-03-1033. Washington, D.C.: September 24, 2003.

Catastrophe Insurance Risks: The Role of Risk-Linked Securities and Factors Affecting Their Use. GAO-02-941. Washington, D.C.: September 24, 2002.

Terrorism Insurance: Rising Uninsured Exposure to Attacks Heightens Potential Economic Vulnerabilities. GAO-02-472T. Washington, D.C.: February 27, 2002.

Terrorism Insurance: Alternative Programs for Protecting Insurance Consumers. GAO-02-199T. Washington, D.C.: October 24, 2001.

Terrorism Insurance: Alternative Programs for Protecting Insurance Consumers. GAO-02-175T. Washington, D.C.: October 24, 2001.

GAO's Mission

The Government Accountability Office, the audit, evaluation, and investigative arm of Congress, exists to support Congress in meeting its constitutional responsibilities and to help improve the performance and accountability of the federal government for the American people. GAO examines the use of public funds; evaluates federal programs and policies; and provides analyses, recommendations, and other assistance to help Congress make informed oversight, policy, and funding decisions. GAO's commitment to good government is reflected in its core values of accountability, integrity, and reliability.

END NOTES

[1] For statistics on the September 11, 2001, terrorist attacks, see Department of the Treasury, Board of Governors of the Federal Reserve System, Securities and Exchange Commission, and Commodity Futures Trading Commission, *Terrorism Risk Insurance: Report of the President's Working Group on Financial Markets* (Washington, D.C.: September 2006), 8.

[2] Charles Meade and Roger C. Molander, *Considering the Effects of a Catastrophic Terrorist Attack* (Santa Monica, Calif.: 2006). This scenario, developed by the RAND Center for Terrorism Risk Management Policy, involved a 10-kiloton nuclear bomb in a shipping container that explodes on the ground, shortly after the container is unloaded onto the pier.

[3] Pub. L. No. 107-297, 116 Stat. 2322 (Nov. 26, 2002). Under TRIA, for 2007 and each year thereafter, the federal government would reimburse participating insurers for 85 percent of their losses up to a specified level, after the insurers pay a deductible equal to 20 percent of an individual insurer's earned premium.

[4] See GAO, *Terrorism Insurance: Measuring and Predicting Losses from Unconventional Weapons Is Difficult, but Some Industry Exposure Exists*, GAO-06-1081 (Washington, D.C.: Sept. 25, 2006). Commercial property/casualty insurance covers physical losses to property, business interruption or loss of the use of buildings due to property damage, and legal liability related to the maintenance of the property and business operations. Workers' compensation insurance covers employees for death or injuries as a result of a workplace incident. Group life insurers sell policies to members of a group, usually employees of the same company or members of the same association, to provide benefits to designated survivors after the death of the insured. Health insurance covers medical expenses resulting from sickness and injury.

[5] Because TRIA requires that insurers offer terrorism coverage that does not "differ materially" from the coverage in the rest of the policy, in their initial offer of terrorism coverage, insurers may not add any additional exclusions or conditional language to the policies specifying any terrorism risk as not being covered. However, representatives of insurers reported that their long-standing exclusions for nuclear and pollution risks generally contained in their commercial property/casualty policies would apply to exclude coverage for NBCR damages caused by terrorist attacks.

[6] TRIA provides federal reinsurance for insured losses only in commercial lines of property and casualty insurance, which includes workers' compensation policies among other things. TRIA does not include health or life insurance. See 15 U.S.C. § 6701 note (Terrorism Insurance Program § 102(12)).

[7] Pub. L. No. 110-160, 121 Stat. 1839 (Dec. 26, 2007).

[8] A pool of insurers provides joint coverage for losses at nuclear power plants.

[9] Captive insurers are generally established by major corporations, such as large real estate companies, to self-insure a variety of risks.

[10] Insurers rely on estimates of the severity (range of damages) and frequency (number of losses in a given time period) to predict expected losses and calculate premiums adequate to cover those losses. For example, insurers have access to large amounts of statistical and historical data on automobile accidents from which they can estimate expected losses; however, for infrequent and potentially catastrophic risks, such as NBCR attacks, insurers have little to no prior experience from which to use in estimating expected losses.

[11] Private workers' compensation insurers are companies that may elect to provide coverage for workers' compensation in a state or for a particular employer. State workers' compensation funds are generally residual market programs established by the state to either (1) accept employers that cannot obtain insurance coverage in the private market or (2) serve as the monopoly or sole provider for workers' compensation insurance coverage in the state.

[12] In prior reports, we have identified and reviewed other options for expanding insurance availability for natural catastrophes and terrorist attacks, such as allowing insurers to set aside tax-deductible reserves for such events, forming risk-sharing pools, or facilitating the issuance of catastrophe bonds through changes in the tax code. While some of these options (such as tax-deductible reserves and risk pools) are also discussed in this chapter, our analysis is in the context of insurers being required to provide NBCR coverage, with the federal government assuming a significant share of the associated financial exposure. The options we reviewed for this chapter were proposed either as initial legislation or by industry participants as a means to help insurers manage any NBCR risks that they would retain. However, given the nature of NBCR risks as discussed in this chapter, in the absence of a mandate that insurers provide NBCR coverage, these other options have limited support. See GAO, *Terrorism Insurance: Status of Efforts by Policyholders to Obtain Coverage,* GAO-08-1057 (Washington, D.C.: Sept. 15, 2008); and *Catastrophe Risk: U.S. and European Approaches to Insure Natural Catastrophe and Terrorism Risks,* GAO-05-199 (Washington, D.C.: Feb. 28, 2005).

[13] The federal share of insured losses under TRIA is 85 percent, with insurers being responsible for a deductible of 20 percent of direct earned premiums as well as a copayment; the proposal would lower the deductible to 3.5 percent for losses resulting from an attack using NBCR materials the first year of the program and raise it incrementally thereafter. See H.R. 2761, 110th Cong. § 3 (2007).

[14] Lloyd Dixon, Robert J. Lempert, Tom LaTourrette, and Robert T. Reville, *The Federal Role in Terrorism Insurance: Evaluating Alternatives in an Uncertain World* (Santa Monica, Calif.: 2007).

[15] NAIC is an organization of state insurance regulators and serves to coordinate regulation of multistate insurers.

[16] GAO-06-1081.

[17] *See* 15 U.S.C. § 6701 note (Terrorism Insurance Program §§ 102(7)(F) and 103(e)(1)(A)). Treasury regulation codified at 31 C.F.R. § 50.5(d), defines "direct earned premium" as "a direct earned premium for all commercial property and casualty insurance issued by any insurer for insurance against all losses, including losses from an act of terrorism, occurring at locations" within the United States or, to U.S. Air Carriers or U.S. flag vessels, or at the premises of any U.S. mission. Treasury provided further clarification that direct earned premiums are "earned as reported to the NAIC in the Annual Statement in column 2 of Exhibit of Premiums and Losses (commonly known as Statutory Page 14)" and cover all risks, not only risks from terrorism.

[18] The Terrorism Risk Insurance Program Reauthorization Act of 2007 clarified language on insurers' liability, stating that insurers are not responsible for losses that exceed an annual liability cap of $100 billion. *See* 15 U.S.C. § 6701 note (Terrorism Insurance Program § 103(e)(2)(A)(i) and (ii)).

[19] H.R. 2761, 110th Cong. § 3 (2007); H.R. 4314, 109th Cong. § 2 (2005).

[20] *Id.*

[21] Texas is an exception; most employers in that state may elect not to have the protections of workers' compensation insurance. In at least 35 states and Washington, D.C., employers may establish high-deductible programs with admitted insurers, where the employer covers losses under a net retention level and the insurer (or insurers) covers any claims above that amount, according to the National Council on Compensation Insurance, Inc. (NCCI).

[22] As of September 30, 2008, and according to NCCI, these states are North Dakota, Ohio, Washington, and Wyoming. In addition, information from AASICF and NCCI indicated that in all but five states, the state fund cannot turn away or limit coverage.

[23] Source: NAIC. In order to self-insure workers' compensation losses, employers must meet certain eligibility requirements proving they are financially able to do so.

[24] In 2005, Treasury reported on results of a national survey of insurers that found, on average, that 35 percent of insurers in TRIA-eligible lines reported they wrote some coverage for NBCR terrorism risks. However, Treasury officials have stated some limitations with this figure, as some insurers responding to the survey may offer NBCR coverage in one commercial property/casualty policy and some may offer in all of their policies. See Department of the Treasury, Report to Congress, *Assessment: The Terrorism Risk Insurance Act of 2002* (Washington, D.C.: June 30, 2005).

[25] *See* Couch on Ins. § 127.8 (2006).

[26] According to information from the Insurance Information Institute and ISO, the states that do not allow exclusions to the Standard Fire Policy for terrorism—thereby requiring coverage for fire following an act of terrorism—are California, Georgia, Hawaii, Illinois, Iowa, Maine, Massachusetts, Missouri, New Jersey, New York, North Carolina, Oregon, Rhode Island, Washington, West Virginia, and Wisconsin. Connecticut and Virginia enable an exclusion of fire following a certified act of terrorism. Fire coverage in both of these states would be required if TRIA expired.

[27] RIMS officials told us they surveyed their deputy members, or the company's highest-ranking individual responsible for making insurance decisions. Deputy members from 377 of 3,500 companies responded to the survey, about a 10 percent response rate. RIMS representatives told us that they could not determine the industry or the size of company the respondents represented.

[28] In addition to one-on-one interviews with policyholders, we conducted group discussions with representatives of 14 policyholders at the annual RIMS conference in San Diego, California, in April 2008.

[29] Under TRIA, insurers required to participate in the program are generally defined as entities, among others, licensed and or admitted to engage in the business of providing primary or excess insurance in any state. *See* 15 U.S.C. § 6701 note (Terrorism Insurance Program § 102(6)(A)(i). Because captives are licensed and admitted by the states, captives may be insurers under TRIA and, therefore, may be eligible for payments for losses related to certified NBCR attacks.

[30] States that allow corporations to set up captives may subject those captives to certain capital and licensing requirements.

[31] Regulatory officials we interviewed were from California, Georgia, Illinois, Massachusetts, New York, and Washington, D.C.

[32] In the United States, the number of terrorist attacks with significant insured losses includes the September 11 attacks, the 1995 Oklahoma City Bombing, and the 1993 World Trade Center bombing, according to the Insurance Information Institute. In addition, as we previously have discussed, a limited number of incidents involving biological agents have occurred in the United States. See GAO/NSIAD-99-163.

[33] See Stephen J. Carroll, Tom LaTourette, Brian G. Chow, Gregory S. Jones, and Craig Martin, *Distribution of Losses from Large Terrorist Attacks Under the Terrorism Risk Insurance Act* (Santa Monica, Calif.: 2005).

The authors concede that their analysis is limited by the sparse history of documented anthrax victims, so that "there is substantial uncertainty about the injury distribution that can be expected in an attack."

[34] AIR, *Proposed NBCR Changes to TRIEA [Terrorism Risk Insurance Extension Act] and Their Impact on Insurers' Terrorism Exposure* (Boston, Mass: October 2007), 1. In addition, we have recently reported that urban plume models that federal agencies have developed specifically for tracking the release of NBCR materials in urban areas have major limitations in terms of predicting the path and the extent of contamination. See GAO-08-180.

[35] Risk Management Solutions, Inc., *Terrorism Risk: 7-Year Retrospective, 7-Year Future Perspective*; RMS White Paper (Newark, Calif.: 2008).

[36] We recently reported that insurers mitigate potential losses from a single, conventional terrorism attack by limiting the amount of property coverage that they would offer in confined geographic areas within cities. Using risk models, insurers map the locations of properties they cover as well as other types of coverage they provide in the area so that they can consider the extent to which one terrorist attack could trigger losses among multiple lines of insurance. See GAO-08-1057.

[37] Private insurers offering workers' compensation insurance policies can decide to which employers to offer coverage, but as we have previously discussed, their workers' compensation policies cannot contain any exclusions for losses from terrorist or NBCR attacks.

[38] Residual market mechanisms called "assigned risk plans" can limit the ability of private workers' compensation insurers to manage NBCR risks in some states. In these states, employers that cannot obtain workers' compensation coverage in the private or "voluntary" market are assigned to private workers' compensation insurers, which administer their claims and share in the funding of those claims. Representatives of one private insurer we contacted told us that with assigned risk policyholders, their company has less information about the type and location of the employer. See also Patricia Danzon and Scott E. Harrington, "Workers' Compensation Rate Regulation: How Price Controls Increase Costs," *Journal of Law and Economics*, vol. 44, no. 1 (April 2001), 5.

[39] One cent per $100 payroll is the average for the voluntary workers' compensation terrorism surcharge. The highest surcharge developed by NCCI is 5 cents per $100 payroll, used in Washington, D.C.

[40] NCCI is an organization that prepares insurance rate (price) recommendations for workers' compensation insurance.

[41] GAO-06-1081.

[42] *See* H.R. 2761, 110th Congress (September 2007). For property/casualty insurance, this deductible would have increased by 50 basis points (0.5 percent) each succeeding program year.

[43] The bill provided for different copayments depending on the amount of losses from an attack. The federal share of compensation for insured losses would have been 85 percent of aggregate industry qualified NBCR losses of less than $10 billion, 87.5 percent for losses from $10 billion to $20 billion, 90.0 percent for losses from $20 billion to $40 billion, 92.5 percent for losses from $40 billion up to $60 billion, and 95.0 percent above $60 billion. In contrast, the federal share of insured losses for terrorist attacks in general is 85.0 percent, regardless of the amount of losses from an attack, up to the $100 billion cap.

[44] Specifically, section 4 of the proposed legislation would have established a Terrorism Buy-Down Fund. Insurers also could have used the premiums reserved in this fund to pay for losses from an attack that did not meet the $100 million TRIA program trigger, which could have benefited smaller insurers.

[45] See *The Federal Role in Terrorism Insurance.* Specifically, the study analyzed the effect of modifying TRIA to require insurers to offer policies that cover NBCR and conventional attacks with a reduced deductible for NBCR attacks and a hard program cap on the total amount of losses for which insurers would be responsible. The analysis in the study suggested that providing for a specific limit on total insurer losses and lowering the deductible were critical to achieving positive outcomes if TRIA were to be modified to require insurers to offer coverage for NBCR terrorist attacks.

[46] The RAND study did not analyze the effect of allowing policyholders to purchase NBCR coverage separately from conventional coverage. However, the authors noted that because existing research suggests overall low demand for NBCR coverage, allowing NBCR coverage to be offered separately might not result in substantial increases in the number of policyholders purchasing such coverage.

[47] The RAND study found that partial government reimbursement of insurer losses in the larger, and they presumed less likely, NBCR attacks would lower prices for NBCR coverage and increase the percentage of businesses purchasing such coverage. The higher rate of businesses purchasing NBCR coverage would reduce government liabilities in the likelier smaller attacks, across a broad range of assumptions about the relative likelihood of large and small attacks and the fraction of uninsured losses that are compensated by the government.

[48] Under current federal tax law, insurers can take a deduction for losses that already have occurred and for setting aside reserves for fair and reasonable estimates of the amount the insurer will be required to pay on future losses. However, reserves for uncertain future losses currently are not tax deductible. Because the size and timing of terrorist attacks are uncertain, any reserves set aside for potential terrorism losses would be taxed as corporate

income in the year in which they were set aside. According to a Treasury official, insurers are permitted to pool coverage under the current TRIA program.

[49] GAO-08-1057 and GAO-05-199.

[50] GAO-08-1057.

[51] The Tillinghast and Reinsurance Businesses of Towers Perrin, *Workers' Compensation Terrorism Reinsurance Pool Feasibility Study, Summary of Study Findings and Conclusions* (March 2004). The study was facilitated by the American Insurance Association and funded by 14 insurers that account for roughly 40 percent of the workers' compensation market.

[52] GAO-08-1057.

[53] For more information on these programs, see GAO, *Natural Disasters: Public Policy Options for Changing the Federal Role in Natural Catastrophe Insurance*, GAO-08-7 (Washington, D.C.: Nov. 26, 2008); *National Flood Insurance Program: Preliminary Views on FEMA's Ability to Ensure Accurate Payments on Hurricane-Damaged Properties*, GAO-07-991T (Washington, D.C.: June 12, 2007); *Federal Emergency Management Agency: Improvements Needed to Enhance Oversight and Management of the National Flood Insurance Program*, GAO-06-119 (Washington, D.C.: Oct. 18, 2005); Crop *Insurance: Actions Needed to Reduce Program's Vulnerability to Fraud, Waste, and Abuse*, GAO-05-528 (Washington, D.C.: Sept. 30, 2005); and *Crop Insurance: Federal Program Faces Insurability and Design Problems*, GAO/RCED-93-98 (Washington, D.C.: May 24, 1993).

[54] In GAO-08-7, we reported that crop insurance subsidies totaled about $2.3 billion in crop years 2005 and 2006, and that flood insurance subsidies total about $1.3 billion annually. We also have reported that to pay $17.7 billion in flood losses from the 2005 Gulf Coast hurricanes, the Federal Emergency Management Agency (FEMA), which administers NFIP, borrowed $17.5 billion from Treasury. As of December 2007, FEMA owed more than $17.3 billion to Treasury. See GAO, *National Flood Insurance Program: Financial Challenges Underscore Need for Improved Oversight of Mitigation Programs and Key Contracts,* GAO-08-437 (Washington, D.C.: June 16, 2008).

[55] GAO-08-7.

[56] GAO-06-1081.

In: Terrorism Insurance
Editor: Miguel H. Palacios

ISBN: 978-1-60741-794-1

Chapter 4

TERRORISM INSURANCE: STATUS OF EFFORTS BY POLICYHOLDERS TO OBTAIN COVERAGE

United States Government Accountability Office

WHY GAO DID THIS STUDY

The Terrorism Risk Insurance Act of 2002 (TRIA) specifies that the federal government assume significant financial responsibility for insured losses on commercial properties resulting from future terrorist attacks. While TRIA has been credited with stabilizing markets for terrorism insurance after the September 11, 2001, attacks, questions remain as to whether certain policyholders, especially those located in large urban areas viewed as being at high risk of attack, may still face challenges in obtaining coverage. GAO was asked to conduct a study to describe (1) whether the availability of terrorism insurance for commercial properties is constrained in any geographic markets, (2) factors limiting insurers' willingness to provide coverage, and (3) advantages and disadvantages of selected public policy options to increase the availability of such insurance.

To address these objectives, GAO analyzed available data and interviewed industry participants, including those with expertise in specific geographic markets considered to be at high, moderate, or low risk of attack (Atlanta, Boston, Chicago, New York, San Francisco, and Washington, D.C.).

GAO provided a draft of this chapter to the Department of the Treasury and the National Association of Insurance Commissioners (NAIC). Treasury and NAIC said the report was informative and useful.

WHAT GAO FOUND

While some owners of high-value properties in major cities may face initial challenges obtaining terrorism insurance coverage compared with most policyholders nationwide, they generally have reported that they could meet current coverage requirements through a variety of approaches. Many industry participants said that terrorism insurance is currently available nationwide at prices viewed as reasonable and that the TRIA program was a key reason for these favorable conditions. However, some policyholders that own large, high-value properties in densely built urban areas viewed as at high risk of attack, particularly in Manhattan and to a lesser extent in Chicago and San Francisco, may still face initial challenges obtaining desired amounts of coverage at prices viewed as reasonable, according to industry participants. To address these challenges, some policyholders purchased coverage from a large number of insurers, which can be a time-consuming and complicated process for policyholders and their insurance brokers. Others purchased coverage in a separate policy (rather than as part of an overall property insurance package) which may be more costly, or self-insured.

While TRIA specifies that the federal government assume substantial financial responsibility for insured losses associated with future terrorist attacks, the steps insurers take to manage the risks they do face appear to be the primary reason some policyholders face challenges in obtaining coverage. Insurers said they seek to mitigate potential terrorism losses by limiting the amount of property coverage that they offered in specific areas of cities, such as downtown locations or areas considered to be at high risk of attack. These risk mitigation efforts generally make obtaining coverage more difficult or costly for policyholders with high-value properties in these areas, according to a variety of sources GAO contacted. Industry participants also said that the availability of reinsurance (insurance for insurers) and the views of rating agencies can limit the availability of coverage in such cities.

Industry participants had no consensus on whether TRIA should be modified or additional actions taken to increase the availability of terrorism coverage, and identified advantages and disadvantages of selected policy proposals that have been included in legislation, discussed in prior GAO reports, or suggested by industry participants to increase such coverage. A proposal to increase the federal government's current responsibility under TRIA for the insured losses associated with a future attack could make insurers more willing to offer coverage in affected areas. For example, one large insurer said that the proposal might make the company more willing to immediately offer additional coverage in cities viewed as at high risk of attack. However, any such benefits might be limited for reasons including the widespread insurance market disruptions that may result from another attack. This proposal, along with several other proposals analyzed in the report, also would increase the federal government's exposure to the losses associated with terrorist attacks, which is already 85 percent of losses up to $100 billion annually, after an industry deductible.

September 15, 2008

The Honorable Christopher J. Dodd
Chairman
The Honorable Richard C. Shelby
Ranking Member
Committee on Banking, Housing, and Urban Affairs
United States Senate

The Honorable Barney Frank
Chairman
The Honorable Spencer Bachus
Ranking Member Committee on Financial Services
House of Representatives

The terrorist attacks of September 11, 2001, are estimated to have resulted in insured losses amounting to $32.5 billion, as of 2006.[1] Subsequent to the attacks, insurers largely stopped offering terrorism insurance coverage to commercial property owners, which raised significant concerns about potential negative economic consequences. For example, existing real estate development projects faced delays and cancellations following September 11 because they could not get terrorism coverage, which led to concerns that the economy, which was already suffering as a result of the attacks, would further deteriorate. To help restore confidence and stability in property insurance markets, Congress enacted and the President signed the Terrorism Risk Insurance Act of 2002 (TRIA).[2] Under TRIA, insurers generally are required to offer terrorism insurance to their commercial clients on the same terms they offer other types of insurance, and, in the event of a future terrorist attack, are responsible for paying a deductible of 20 percent of their direct earned premiums from the previous year to cover related losses.[3] The federal government is responsible for covering 85 percent of the insured losses up to a maximum of $100 billion on an annual basis after insurance companies pay the deductible. While TRIA, which was reauthorized in 2005 and again in 2007, generally has been credited with stabilizing markets for commercial property insurance, some building owners, Members of Congress, and others remain concerned that there may still be gaps in coverage.[4] In particular, they have expressed concerns about the ability of policyholders that are located in large urban areas viewed as being at high risk of attack to obtain terrorism insurance coverage.

To assist the committees in their oversight efforts of the insurance industry, you asked that we conduct a study to determine if specific markets in the United States have any unique constraints on the amount of terrorism insurance available and evaluate options to enhance coverage. As agreed with your staff, we are providing a report that describes (1) whether the availability of terrorism insurance for commercial properties is constrained in any geographic markets and the effect of any constraints on pricing and coverage amounts, (2) factors limiting insurers' willingness to provide coverage, and (3) advantages and disadvantages of some public policy options to increase the availability of property terrorism insurance.[5]

To assess whether the availability of terrorism insurance for commercial properties is constrained in any geographic markets, we compiled and analyzed available data on insurance and reinsurance companies, terrorism insurance take-up rates, and terrorism insurance pricing.[6] We also interviewed more than 100 industry participants with nationwide perspective and expertise in specific geographic markets, including Atlanta, Boston, Chicago, New York, San Francisco, and Washington, D.C. We selected these high-, moderate-, and low-risk markets based on an industry analyst's ranking of cities by risk of terrorism. Our interviews included insurer and policyholder trade associations, policyholders in a variety of industries, national and regional insurance and reinsurance brokers, insurance and reinsurance companies, and state regulators. To identify the factors that may contribute to insurers' willingness or ability to provide terrorism insurance coverage, we selected large, national insurance companies to interview based on their market share in the states we studied. These national insurance companies held from 37 to 52 percent of the market share in the states we studied. In addition, we interviewed representatives of regional insurance companies in our selected markets. We also spoke with risk modeling firms and credit rating agencies. To obtain views on the advantages and disadvantages of some public policy options that have been proposed in legislation, discussed in our prior reports, or suggested by industry participants to increase insurers' capacity (that is, their willingness or ability) to provide terrorism coverage, we relied on our interviews with industry participants described above. We also interviewed academics who have written on the topic of terrorism insurance, research organizations, and consumer interest groups. Although we selected industry participants to provide broad representation of market conditions geographically and by industry, the number of participants may not necessarily be representative of the universe of insurers, insurance brokers, policyholders, and regulators. As a result, we could not generalize the results of our analysis to the entire national market for commercial property terrorism insurance. Appendix I contains additional details of our objectives, scope, and methodology.

We conducted our audit in California, Georgia, Illinois, Massachusetts, New York, and Washington, D.C., from January 2008 to September 2008, in accordance with generally accepted government auditing standards. Those standards require that we plan and perform the audit to obtain sufficient, appropriate evidence to provide a reasonable basis for our findings and conclusions based on our audit objectives. We believe that the evidence obtained provides a reasonable basis for our findings and conclusions based on our audit objectives.

Results in Brief

While some owners of high-value properties in major cities may face initial challenges obtaining desired amounts of terrorism coverage compared to most policyholders nationwide, they generally have reported being able to meet their current coverage requirements through a variety of approaches. Many industry participants and policyholders said that terrorism insurance currently is available nationwide at prices viewed as reasonable, and they cited the TRIA program and the current "soft," or competitive, insurance market for these generally favorable conditions. However many industry participants also said that certain policyholders, especially those seeking large policies in areas viewed as at higher risk of terrorist attack, may face initial challenges obtaining full coverage for terrorism at rates viewed as reasonable. According to policyholders and brokers, these policyholders typically own large, high-value properties such as office towers or hotels in urban areas where many large buildings are clustered and that are viewed as at high risk of attack, particularly in Manhattan, and to a lesser extent certain areas of other major cities such as Chicago and San Francisco. To address these challenges and satisfy their current coverage requirements, policyholders and insurance brokers we contacted reported adopting one or more of several different approaches. For example, some policyholders purchased coverage from a larger number of insurers in complex insurance programs, adding to what can be a time-consuming and complicated process for the policyholders and their brokers. Moreover, some policyholders purchased coverage in a separate terrorism-only policy (rather than including the coverage in their standard all-risk property insurance package) for a portion or all of their insurance needs, which may be more costly than the traditional approach. Other policyholders, typically large corporations, self-insured a portion or all of their terrorism coverage requirements through what are known as "captive" insurance companies that have been set up to insure the risks of their owners.

While TRIA limits insurers' financial exposure in future terrorist attacks, several insurers said they remained concerned about the exposure they retained, and their efforts to minimize potential losses appear to be a primary reason why some policyholders faced challenges in obtaining coverage. Insurers said they seek to mitigate potential losses from a single terrorism attack by limiting the amount of property coverage that they offer in specific areas of cities, such as downtowns or financial districts where many large buildings are clustered, or other areas considered to be at high risk of attack, such as parts of Manhattan. These exposure limits, referred to here as aggregation limits, generally make obtaining coverage more difficult or costly for certain policyholders in these areas, according to a variety of sources we contacted. For instance, an insurer could decline to cover a property in a certain area, offer a lower coverage amount, or charge a higher premium rate. Industry participants also said the limited availability of reinsurance (insurance for insurers) and the views of credit rating agencies can affect the availability and cost of terrorism insurance in cities viewed as at high risk of attack. Reinsurers we contacted said that they also have established aggregation limits in certain cities to mitigate their risks, and rating agency officials said that their credit ratings for insurers often depend, in part, on their ability to manage the potential losses associated with terrorist attacks in major urban areas.

Insurance industry participants and analysts we contacted had no consensus on whether TRIA should be modified or additional actions taken to increase the availability of terrorism insurance coverage. They also identified advantages and disadvantages of various policy proposals that have been made in legislation, discussed in our prior reports, or suggested by industry participants to increase terrorism coverage. For example, one recent legislative proposal involves lowering the TRIA deductible to 5 percent (from 20 percent) for insurers experiencing losses from a future terrorist attack that results in more than $1 billion in damages. Supporters of this proposal argue that lowering the TRIA deductible could make insurers more willing to offer coverage following an attack, which would stabilize insurance markets in affected areas and facilitate rebuilding and recovery efforts. In addition, a large insurer said that the legislative proposal, if adopted, might make it immediately more willing to offer terrorism insurance coverage to policyholders in certain cities where some policyholders currently face initial challenges in obtaining coverage. While not necessarily opposed to the proposal, other industry participants and analysts cautioned that its effects may be limited. For example, they said that several large insurers already seek to manage their potential losses from a potential terrorist attack, through aggregation limits, to levels well below the current TRIA deductible of 20 percent. As a result, even lowering the deductible to 5 percent would not necessarily result in a significant increase in the coverage offered by such insurers. Further, insurance market disruptions associated with another terrorist attack could limit the supply and cost of coverage even if the federal government assumed greater responsibility for such losses. Industry participants also identified both advantages and disadvantages associated with other proposals to increase terrorism insurance availability. The proposals are: permitting insurers to establish tax-deductible reserves for terrorism-related loses, forming a group of insurers to pool assets for terrorism risks, facilitating the use of catastrophe bonds for terrorism through amendments to the federal tax code, and limiting certain state regulation of property insurance premiums or amending coverage requirements.

We note that while several of these proposals (for example, establishing tax-deductible reserves) might enhance the availability and price of terrorism coverage, any such effects likely would take place over the longer term and not immediately address challenges that certain policyholders initially may face in obtaining coverage. Further, all of the proposals, except amending state regulations, also could increase the federal government's exposure to potential terrorism-related losses or otherwise reduce federal revenues.

We provided a draft of this chapter to the Department of the Treasury and the National Association of Insurance Commissioners (NAIC) for their review and comment. In oral comments, Department of the Treasury and NAIC officials said that they found the report informative and useful. They also provided technical comments that were incorporated where appropriate.

Background

TRIA requires private insurers to offer terrorism coverage in commercial property and casualty insurance, including workers' compensation insurance policies. Insurers must make terrorism coverage available to their policyholders on the same terms and conditions, including coverage levels, as other types of insurance coverage. For example, an insurer offering $100 million in commercial property coverage must offer $100 million in coverage for property damage from a certified terrorist attack.[7] However, insurers could impose an additional charge for the coverage and policyholders, except in workers' compensation policies, generally have the option of not purchasing it.

Under TRIA, the federal government is to reimburse insurers for a portion of their losses from certified terrorist acts. Specifically, the federal government would reimburse insurers for 85 percent of their losses after the insurers pay a deductible amounting to 20 percent of the previous year's direct earned premiums.[8] The federal funding is activated when aggregate industry losses exceed $100 million and is capped at an annual amount of $100 billion.[9]

Originally enacted as a 3-year program, Congress has reauthorized the program twice and recently extended it until 2014. In December 2005, Congress passed the Terrorism Risk Insurance Extension Act that increased the required amount insurers would have to pay in the aftermath of a terrorist attack. In December 2007, Congress approved the Terrorism Risk Insurance Program Reauthorization Act and eliminated the distinction between terrorist acts carried out by foreign and domestic actors. It also clarified language on insurers' liability, stating that insurers are not responsible for losses that exceed the federal government's annual liability cap of $100 billion.[10]

Commercial property insurance policies can be simple or complex, depending on the value and location of the properties being insured. Property owners may insure properties individually or consolidate multiple properties in a portfolio and insure them with a single policy. The benefits of grouping properties include spreading the cost (premium) across more than one building on the premise that all buildings in a portfolio are unlikely to be damaged by the same peril in the same event. Policies with high insured values can require multiple insurers to provide coverage, with each providing a portion of the coverage up to the full amount of the policy, because the total insured value is too great for any one insurer to absorb (see Figure 1). According to a representative of a large brokerage firm, policyholders typically buy property coverage, including terrorism coverage, through one all-risk policy, which insures losses from multiple perils.

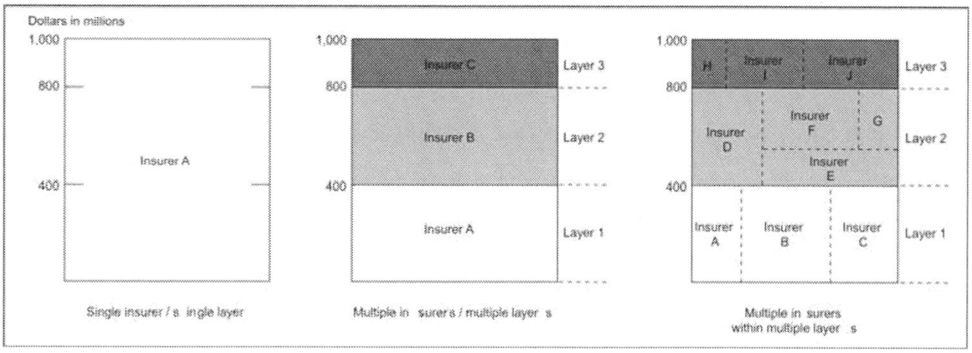

Figure 1. Examples of Structuring Options for Commercial Property Insurance

Source: GAO

Policyholders generally do not purchase terrorism insurance in amounts that would cover the total replacement value of the insured property, but rather purchase insurance in amounts that reflect the maximum amount of foreseeable losses that could occur in a terrorist attack. Also, policyholders may determine the amount of terrorism coverage to purchase based on amounts required by a lender providing the mortgage on the property.

States have primary responsibility for regulating the insurance industry in the United States, and state insurance regulators coordinate their activities in part through the NAIC. The degree of oversight of insurance varies by state and insurance type. In some lines of insurance, insurers may file insurance policy forms with state regulators that help determine the extent of coverage provided by a policy by approving the wording of policies, including the explicit exclusions of some perils. According to a NAIC representative, while practices vary by state, state regulators generally regulate prices for personal lines of insurance and workers' compensation policies but not for commercial property/casualty policies. In most cases, state insurance regulators perform neither rate nor form review for large commercial property/casualty insurance contracts because it is presumed that businesses have a better understanding of insurance contracts and pricing than the average personal-lines consumer. Reinsurers generally are not required to get state regulatory approval for the terms of coverage or the prices they charge.

Terrorism Insurance Generally is available Nationwide, although some Policyholders had to take Additional Steps to Obtain Coverage

According to a variety of sources, commercial property terrorism insurance currently appears to be widely available on a nationwide basis at rates viewed as reasonable, largely due to the TRIA program and the current "soft" insurance market. However, some policyholders in urban areas viewed as being at higher risk of a terrorist attack, particularly in

Manhattan and to a lesser extent in some other high-risk cities such as Chicago and San Francisco, may be forced to take additional steps to overcome challenges they may have initially faced in obtaining desired amounts of coverage at prices viewed as reasonable. Policyholders generally have been able to obtain desired or required amounts of terrorism coverage by increasing the number of carriers in what already may be large and complex insurance programs, adding to what can be a time-consuming and complicated process for policyholders and their insurance brokers. Others secure needed coverage by purchasing all or a portion of their terrorism coverage in a separate insurance policy, or self-insuring through a captive insurance company.

Terrorism Insurance Generally is Available Nationwide at Rates Viewed as Affordable Largely Due to the TRIA Program and the Soft Insurance Market

According to data compiled by two large insurance brokers, a majority of their commercial clients nationwide purchase terrorism insurance coverage, and the premium rates for such coverage generally have been stable in recent years. As shown in figure 2, one of these brokers reported that approximately 60 percent of its clients purchased some form of terrorism coverage each year from 2005 through 2007. Another large insurance broker reported that take-up rates for its large property clients have remained between 60 percent and 65 percent since 2004. According to a large broker, the Northeast, which includes New York City, has the largest percentage of companies that purchase terrorism coverage for properties, with about 70 percent having purchased it in 2007.[11] Real estate companies account for the largest percentage of clients that purchased terrorism insurance coverage, with more than 80 percent of these clients having done so in 2007. Manufacturing and construction companies had the lowest purchase rates, with 45 percent and 34 percent, respectively, having purchased coverage in 2007. Data collected by one of these large brokers also show that the premiums that their clients paid for terrorism coverage, expressed as a percentage of the commercial property premiums, generally have been stable at around 4 percent since 2003 (fig. 2). Another large broker also reported that premiums have been stable at around 4 percent, on average, since 2006.

An official from one of these brokerages told us steady purchase rates between 2005 and 2007 may indicate that policyholders who want to purchase terrorism coverage have been able to purchase it. According to representatives from these two brokers, the primary reason why approximately 40 percent of clients did not purchase terrorism coverage is that they may not have perceived themselves at risk of a terrorist attack, particularly those in nonurban areas or those in industries perceived to be at lower risk of attack, such as manufacturing. Other reasons clients may not have purchased coverage include the absence of lender requirements or the cost of coverage, according to one large broker.[12]

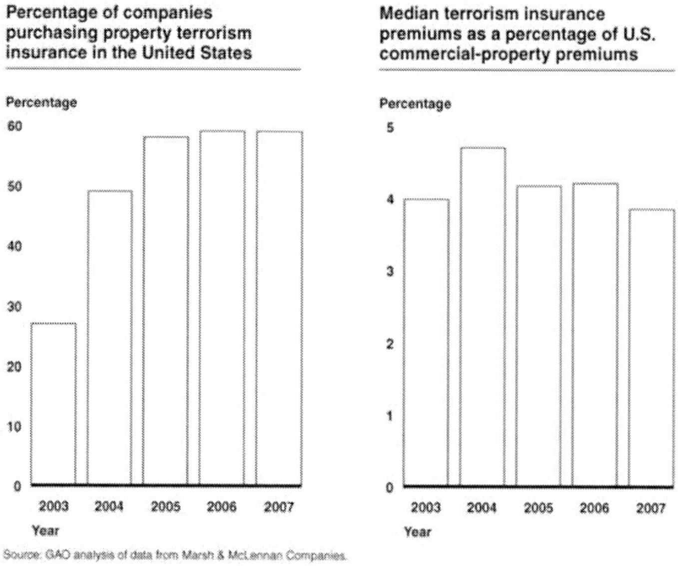

Figure 2. Purchase and Cost Rates of Property Terrorism Insurance

Information we collected in a range of interviews with policyholders, national and regional brokers, insurers, and others was consistent with the view that terrorism insurance coverage is available nationwide at premium rates viewed as reasonable. Several policyholders we contacted that own large and small portfolios of real estate throughout the United States, including national hotel chains, sports stadiums, office towers, shopping malls, and residential buildings, told us they could obtain as much terrorism coverage as they sought to obtain. Some policyholders and regional brokers also said that terrorism insurance premiums continue to decline while the quality of coverage improves. For example, a representative from a commercial real estate company that owns large office towers, a luxury resort, and an industrial property in major U.S. cities said the company recently increased its terrorism coverage by more than 50 percent and decreased its premium by more than 20 percent. In at least one state, an insurer and state regulator told us terrorism coverage may be provided at no additional cost to policyholders, especially those with properties perceived to be at low risk of a terrorist attack.

Insurers, policyholders, and other industry participants cited the TRIA program and the current soft, or competitive, market as the key reasons that terrorism coverage generally has been available nationwide. Without the federal backstop for potential insurance losses related to terrorism, industry participants said that coverage availability could decline substantially. For example, some insurers told us the amount of terrorism coverage they provide would decline—by more than 95 percent for one insurer—without the TRIA provision that provides reimbursement for insured losses that exceed the amount of an insurer's TRIA deductible. In a soft market, insurance is widely available and sold at a lower cost, making it easier for buyers to obtain insurance. According to insurance industry participants, recent strong profits, increases in investment income, and a lack of large losses from major catastrophes have contributed to insurers' ability to increase their capital levels in recent years. According to some brokers, high levels of capital have increased insurers' capacity and willingness to provide terrorism insurance coverage.

However, some interviewees cautioned that another terrorist attack or "hardening" of the general terrorism insurance market could reduce the current supply of terrorism insurance coverage and increase pricing. In the past, insurers frequently have responded to catastrophic events by cutting back coverage significantly or substantially increasing premiums for policyholders. For example, such reactions took place in the Florida market after Hurricane Andrew in 1992, in California after the Northridge earthquake of 1994, and more widely following the September 11 attacks. A broker with a large national firm told us that the insurance industry has remained highly sensitive to the potential financial consequences of another terrorist attack since September 11. According to one industry analyst, even a modest terrorist attack in the future could cause significant fear and concern in the market and lead to increases in prices and restrictions on availability. Moreover, some industry analysts said that insurers could suffer significant losses for a variety of other reasons, such as the costs of a large hurricane or earthquake or declines in the values of their investment portfolios, which might make them less willing to offer terrorism coverage under current terms and pricing.

Some Policyholders in Major Cities Have Faced Initial Challenges in Obtaining Desired Terrorism Coverage at Rates Viewed as Favorable

While terrorism insurance coverage generally is available nationwide, many industry participants reported that some policyholders in major cities viewed as being at higher risk of terrorist attack, particularly in Manhattan, may initially experience challenges in obtaining desired amounts of coverage.[13] Specifically, industry participants said that owners of large, high-value properties in financial districts or downtown locations, or near government offices or transit hubs, may face initial challenges in obtaining coverage in their all-risk property policies. For example, a policyholder with large office and retail properties in New York, San Francisco, and Chicago told us only a few insurers were willing to offer it coverage that it considered expensive and that provided only half of the $1.5 billion in coverage sought. In spite of these initial challenges, this policyholder was able to obtain the needed coverage by taking other approaches that will be discussed later in this chapter.

Brokers and policyholders mentioned these difficulties have been more severe in certain locations in Manhattan than anywhere else. In particular, they said the area surrounding Times Square—or midtown—and lower Manhattan, which contained the World Trade Center, presents difficulties because of the dense concentration of buildings, perceived risk of a future terrorist attack, and the overlapping insurance needs of building owners and tenants. For example, one broker active in the New York market told us of an approximately 15-block stretch of midtown Manhattan with a high concentration of property values in which each property is valued at $1 billion or more, creating strong demand by building owners for limited and expensive coverage. Another broker told us the availability of terrorism coverage is most constrained in the area surrounding the World Trade Center site in lower Manhattan. The brokers said retail clients that would like to establish themselves in this area worry about not enough coverage being available for terrorism, flood, and fire damage.

Representatives from large national brokers, as well as insurance companies and other industry participants, said that certain policyholders in Chicago and San Francisco also may face initial challenges in obtaining terrorism insurance coverage, although to a lesser extent than in Manhattan. As is the case in Manhattan, these policyholders typically own large buildings in proximity to other buildings and generally are located in financial districts or downtown locations. While owners of large buildings in such locations may face challenges in obtaining coverage, a broker told us that even a small building might be difficult to insure for terrorism risk if it were located near larger properties in high-risk areas.

Many industry participants reported that premiums were higher in cities considered to face greater financial risks from the likelihood of terrorist attacks occurring there, adding to the challenge of obtaining terrorism coverage. For example, according to one large insurance broker, terrorism insurance premiums in New York City can be twice as high as prices for similar buildings in other cities considered to be at high risk of a terrorist attack, and more than five times higher than prices in lower-risk cities. The premium amount dedicated to insuring properties in certain locations against terrorism risks may, on a relative basis, significantly exceed the amount necessary to cover such risks in other geographic areas. For example, a broker in the San Francisco Bay area told us average terrorism pricing for owners of certain buildings there can be from 20 to 30 percent of the all-risk property premium, whereas the national median was around 4 percent in 2007.

While some policyholders in high-risk cities face challenges, we note that this is not necessarily the case in all such cities. In particular, policyholders we contacted with properties in Washington D.C. said while it may have been difficult or more expensive to obtain terrorism coverage immediately following September 11, coverage is now readily available and affordable. For example, policyholders we interviewed that own properties in the city said they were able to include full terrorism coverage in their all-risk property policies even though they own or manage commercial and residential properties in proximity to potential targets such as the White House, the Capitol, subway stops, or foreign embassies. Industry participants said that policyholders generally experience fewer challenges in Washington, D.C. because the buildings are not as high or as densely concentrated as in downtown areas of other high-risk cities.

To Obtain Full Terrorism Coverage, Policyholders May Add Additional Carriers to Existing Insurance Programs, Purchase Terrorism-only Policies, or Self-Insure

Policyholders that have experienced initial difficulty obtaining terrorism coverage in their primary all-risk property policies generally have been able to meet current terrorism insurance requirements by one of several approaches or a combination thereof, according to industry participants. For example, some policyholders and brokers reported obtaining coverage from a greater number of insurers in what may already have been a complex insurance program. As discussed earlier, policies with high insured values can require multiple insurers to provide portions of coverage up to the full amount of the policy. However, a few policyholders told us more insurers are now required to assemble terrorism coverage because insurers are taking smaller amounts of risk (that is, offering smaller amounts of coverage), requiring a greater number of insurers to fill out an insurance program and adding to what can be a time-consuming and complicated process for policyholders and their insurance brokers. Some policyholders said more than 20 insurers may participate in a single insurance program. One policyholder told us more than 40 insurers participate in its property insurance policy. Layering an insurance program has costs, especially for large and complex programs. A representative of a large hotel chain told us that layering insurance is "painful" because of the effort involved in convincing insurers to become comfortable with a risk.

Moreover, several brokers and policyholders reported purchasing property terrorism insurance in a stand-alone policy to cover portions or all of the required coverage.[14] For example, the owner of multiple large office buildings in Manhattan's midtown and downtown financial districts told us the company purchased all of its terrorism coverage as a stand-alone insurance policy because it could obtain just half of the $800 million in coverage sought. Another policyholder that owns a nationwide chain of hotels, with properties in Manhattan, Chicago, and San Francisco, decided to purchase all of its terrorism coverage in a stand-alone policy to avoid the high and inconsistent cost of embedding terrorism coverage in its all-risk policy. A representative of this policyholder noted that cost was a particular issue following the 2005 hurricane season when property insurance prices generally increased. Some policyholders told us stand-alone terrorism coverage was more expensive than obtaining coverage as part of an all-risk property policy. However, data from a national broker show that the difference in pricing between stand-alone coverage and coverage included in an all-risk policy was small for most of 2007, with the median price for stand-alone coverage at 5 percent of the overall property premium compared to around 4 percent for coverage in the all-risk program.

Finally, according to brokers and policyholders some policyholders have used self-insurance as a means to assemble coverage. That is, they placed all or a portion of their terrorism coverage in a captive insurance company, which insures the risks of the owner.[15] For the purpose of insuring property terrorism risk, a captive insurer would generally be a wholly owned insurance company within the corporate structure of the property owner. The typical owners of captives used for insuring terrorism risk are large corporations that own large or well-known buildings in major urban areas and have not been able to obtain coverage through other means. For example, a policyholder we contacted sought to obtain $1.2 billion in property coverage for multiple buildings in Manhattan, including terrorism coverage, which would cover the total replacement cost of the largest building in its portfolio.[16] However, a representative of this policyholder told us the company could obtain just $500 million of all-risk property insurance that included terrorism coverage, leaving a gap of $700 million in coverage for terrorism risk. The policyholder considered filling the gap by obtaining terrorism coverage in the form of a more expensive stand-alone insurance policy, but decided instead to establish a captive insurance company to supplement the coverage provided in the all-risk policy and make up the $700 million difference. Another policyholder with a lender requirement to purchase about $1.6 billion in coverage on a single building in midtown Manhattan was unable to obtain sufficient terrorism coverage in an all-risk policy in 2008. This policyholder purchased an all-risk policy that excluded terrorism risk and assembled property coverage for terrorism risk in the form of a $250 million stand-alone policy and about $1.3 billion in a newly formed captive insurance company. Although these examples show policyholders may create captive insurance companies for the sole purpose of insuring terrorism risk, this approach may not be typical of the way in which captives are used.[17] Representatives of two large insurance brokers said most companies simply add terrorism risk to captives that already have been established to cover other insurance risks, such as environmental and product-recall risks.

Insurer and Reinsurer Efforts to Mitigate Their Risks Appeared to be Why Certain Policyholders Faced Initial Challenges in Obtaining Terrorism Insurance Coverage

While TRIA limits insurers' potential losses from a terrorist attack, the efforts of insurers' to manage the remaining risks they faced appeared to be the primary reasons for certain policyholders experiencing initial challenges in obtaining desired amounts of coverage at prices they viewed as reasonable. To mitigate their risks, many insurers set limits on the amount of coverage that they would provide to policyholders in confined geographic areas within a city, such as downtown locations or financial districts where many large buildings are clustered, or in specific areas of cities considered to be at high risk of attack. According to a variety of sources we contacted, these limits generally make obtaining coverage more difficult or costly for certain policyholders in these areas. Further, industry participants and analysts said that the availability of reinsurance and the views of credit rating agencies also may limit the supply and increase the price of terrorism insurance coverage in certain high-risk cities.

Insurers' Concerns about Amounts of Future Terrorism Losses Influence Their Willingness to Provide Coverage, Affecting Availability and Price in Certain Cities

Representatives from several insurance companies we contacted said that despite the TRIA financial backstop, they remain significantly concerned that a future terrorist attack would result in substantial losses. In the event of another terrorist attack, industry participants said that certain large insurers may face TRIA deductibles that would result in losses of billions of dollars. For example, one of the largest insurers providing commercial property coverage would face a $5 billion TRIA deductible based on 2007 data. The representative of one large insurer said that the company's TRIA deductible was three times the net losses the company suffered due to the September 11 attacks. Furthermore, even a terrorist attack that caused losses below the $100 million TRIA program trigger could cause substantial losses to a small insurer. For example, the company surplus might be exhausted from paying the entire loss, according to the representative of a small insurer.[18]

Insurers said that they seek to mitigate potential losses from a single terrorism attack by limiting the amount of property coverage that they offer in confined geographic areas within cities. For example, some insurers told us that they would not insure certain types of properties, buildings over a certain size, or buildings near others that might be considered terrorist targets. In addition, several large insurers and brokers told us that insurers limit the terrorism insurance they provide in these areas to amounts well below their TRIA deductible.

To help insurers determine how much risk, or coverage, they can write in any given location, several industry participants we interviewed said insurers often use computer models to estimate the effect, or severity, of terrorist attacks on their existing book of business. Using models available from risk-modeling firms, insurers can map the locations of properties they cover as well as other types of coverage they provide in the area such as building contents, business interruption, or workers' compensation. Therefore, insurers can consider the extent to which one terrorist attack could trigger losses among multiple lines of insurance. The models also can map the locations of nearby properties considered to be potential terrorist targets. With these mapped locations, an insurer is then able to identify areas where it has the greatest aggregated exposure within a city. The modeling program places a circle around a specific location, such as a building in the insurer's book or a potential terrorist target, and aggregates the amount of exposure an insurer has within this defined area. These models take into account the severity of various attack scenarios on properties in the area (for example, a 5- or 10-ton truck bomb) and allow users to quantify potential losses under different attack scenarios.

Insurers we interviewed noted that they are not as comfortable with the estimates of the probability, or frequency, of an attack, from these models and, therefore, make more limited use of this information. While insurers and risk-modeling firms have access to large historical databases and scientific studies of the frequency and severity of natural catastrophes, such as hurricanes, the data on terrorist attacks are limited. Furthermore, according to industry analysts, the tactics, strength, and effectiveness of terrorist groups can be very unpredictable, so predicting the frequency of such attacks is very difficult and perhaps impossible. For example, terrorists might respond to increased security measures in one area by shifting attention to more vulnerable targets in another. Without more information, industry analysts note that it is difficult for modeling firms to make projections about the capability and opportunities of terrorists to undertake future attacks.

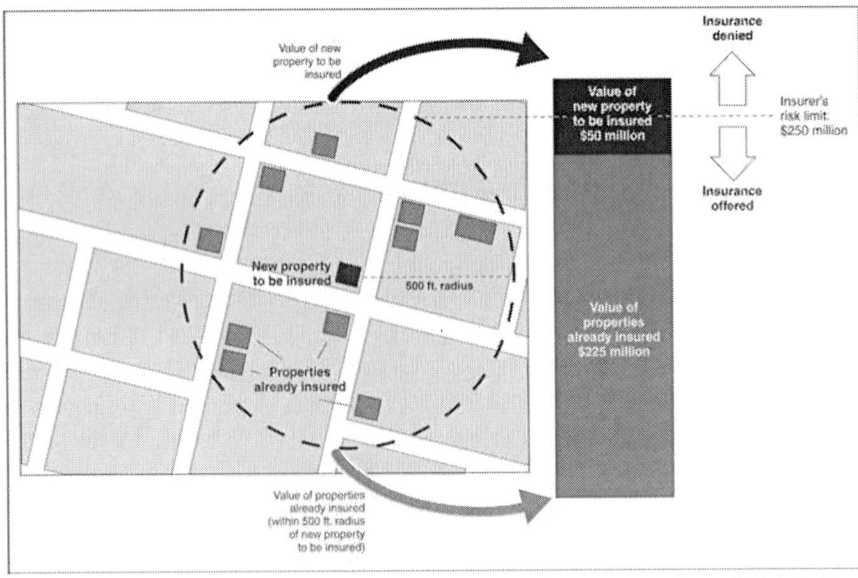

Figure 3. Example of an Insurer's Underwriting Decision Based on Aggregation of Risk in Small, Defined Areas

Source: GAO.

While insurers find estimates of the probability of a terrorist attack of limited use, they often use the estimates of the severity of potential attacks in determining the amount of coverage they are willing to provide. Considering potential attack scenarios and estimated losses from the models, insurers impose internal limits, referred to here as aggregation limits, on the amount of all types of coverage they will offer in defined areas. Depending on the amount of capital and risk tolerance of the company, insurers determine the amount of coverage they are willing to provide in defined geographic areas within a city, such as in 250-foot, 500-foot, or quarter-mile circles around certain landmarks or areas where the insurer has high concentrations of risk. Insurers then monitor the amount of coverage that they provide in these areas on an ongoing basis to ensure that they do not exceed their aggregation limits. As shown in figure 3, an insurer might decline to provide any coverage for a new property since adding the property to the book of business would exceed the insurer's aggregation limit on exposures within the defined area. Alternatively, an insurer might charge a higher price or offer a lower coverage limit if adding the property would exceed the aggregation limit.

The amount of coverage insurers are willing to provide in these defined areas may change frequently as new clients or properties are added to or removed from their books of business. An insurer may have available capacity in a specific area one month, but be near its limit the next. For example, one policyholder noted that her real estate investment company contacts its insurer before considering acquiring a new property to determine if the insurer has capacity where the new property is located. Although the insurance company may decide it can provide property insurance for the building at the time of the request, the policyholder said that when the acquisition is completed several months later, the insurance company may no longer have the capacity available to insure the building. In that case, the policyholder said that the company might have to purchase a stand-alone terrorism policy for that particular building, which the policyholder reported as being more expensive than simply adding it to the existing portfolio. As a result, the policyholder said it might no longer be profitable for the company to acquire the new building. In some cases, this policyholder said the company has canceled or deferred an acquisition until it simultaneously disposed of a building in the same area to be sure that the insurer would have capacity available for the new building. However, several other policyholders we interviewed said that any concern about the availability of insurance has not affected their companies' acquisitions or development projects.

Availability of Reinsurance Also Can Affect Insurers' Willingness to Provide Terrorism Coverage

Insurers and other industry analysts cited the limited availability of reinsurance as another factor influencing insurers' willingness to provide terrorism coverage in certain areas. Reinsurance plays a crucial role in insurance markets by permitting primary insurers to transfer some of the risks that they incur in offering coverage. In so doing, reinsurance may allow primary insurers to offer additional coverage than otherwise would be the case while mitigating potential losses.[19]

Insurers and other industry participants we contacted said that reinsurance for terrorism risk, which largely was unavailable after September 11, continues to be expensive and available in limited amounts. In a 2004 report, we found that reinsurers had reentered the terrorism insurance market cautiously, but that the amount of coverage offered to primary insurers was limited and the premium rates were viewed as high.[20] In conducting our current work, reinsurers and industry analysts said that reinsurance capacity for terrorism has continued to increase for a variety of reasons including an influx of new capital into the industry, the absence of another terrorist attack, and improvements in insurers' ability to underwrite the risk.[21] However, insurance brokers and large insurers with significant exposures in urban areas told us that terrorism often still is excluded in reinsurance contracts and that insurers have been able to purchase only limited amounts of very expensive coverage. A recent Congressional Budget Office report similarly found that the ability of primary insurers to transfer terrorism risk to reinsurers is limited.[22]

As has been the case with primary insurers, the efforts of reinsurers to manage their aggregation levels appear to be why the coverage that they offer for terrorism is limited. The provision in TRIA requiring insurers to offer terrorism coverage at terms and conditions that do not differ materially from other coverage does not apply to reinsurance transactions, so these companies have discretion in deciding how much terrorism coverage to offer to primary companies. Reinsurance company representatives told us that the location of the insured risks is an important factor that influences whether they will offer reinsurance and at what price. For example, one reinsurance company representative said that the company was less willing to write contracts covering properties in cities viewed to be at high risk of terrorist attack. Others said that while their companies still would be willing to reinsure an insurer's book of business with concentrations of risk in multiple high-risk cities, they might offer more expensive coverage to compensate for the increased risk and the increased capital they need to maintain to back up the risk.

Views of Rating Agencies Also May Influence the Availability of Terrorism Insurance for Some Policyholders in Areas Viewed as at High Risk of Attack

Insurers and reinsurers cited the views of rating agencies on the amount of capital insurers allocate to terrorism risk and the location of risks they insure as other factors influencing their willingness to provide terrorism coverage. Rating agencies assess the financial strength of companies and the credit quality of their obligations. Maintaining a high rating can be very important for an insurance company's business because a firm with a low rating may, among other things, pay a higher interest rate on its debt. In addition, several policyholders and lenders told us many lenders that require their mortgagees to carry terrorism coverage also require that they use only highly rated insurers. A variety of industry participants and analysts told us that rating agencies' views can be very influential on the amount of capacity insurers decide to allocate to terrorism risk, affecting how much coverage they provide to policyholders. For example, one reinsurance industry analyst noted that the amount of capital rating agencies required insurers to maintain to support terrorism risk was significant. The representative said that these requirements may encourage insurers not to offer this type of business because it is difficult to maintain large amounts of capital and earn an adequate return on the money.

In conducting their assessments, representatives of the rating agencies we interviewed said they look closely at insurers' terrorism exposures. They request specific information about the types of policies insurers write, the risks in their books of business, the steps insurers take to manage their risks, and whether they have concentrations of risk in any areas, including large urban areas or cities considered to be high risk. With workers'-compensation insurers, the rating agencies request information about the number of employees at different locations across the different insureds. As a result of discussions with the rating agency about the company's rating, rating agency representatives said that some companies have purchased additional reinsurance or divested risk.

Various Proposals to Increase the Availability and Affordability of Terrorism Insurance Coverage Have Both Advantages and Disadvantages

Insurance industry participants and analysts did not express consensus on whether TRIA should be modified or additional actions taken to increase the availability of terrorism insurance coverage. They cited a variety of advantages and disadvantages associated with five proposals that have been offered in legislation, discussed in our prior reports, or suggested by industry participants to increase the availability and perhaps limit the cost of terrorism insurance. These proposals include lowering insurers' TRIA deductibles following large terrorist attacks, permitting insurers to establish tax-deductible reserves for future terrorism losses, forming a group of insurance companies to pool assets for terrorism losses, facilitating the issuance of onshore catastrophe bonds through changes in the tax code, and limiting certain state regulations and requirements. We note that improvements in terrorism insurance coverage and pricing that might result from the adoption of some of these proposals (such as tax-deductible reserves, insurance pools, and catastrophe bonds) likely would take place over the longer term and that such proposals could increase the federal government's exposure to terrorist-related losses or otherwise reduce federal revenues.

Option 1: Lowering Insurers' TRIA Deductibles following Large Terrorist Attacks

One recent legislative proposal to increase the availability of terrorism insurance coverage involved lowering the TRIA deductible for insurers from future terrorist attacks after they experience losses.[23] Under this proposal, if there were a terrorist attack that resulted in more than $1 billion in damages, the insurer deductible under TRIA immediately would be reduced to 5 percent (from 20 percent) for those insurers suffering losses in the attack.[24] Table 1 below shows the potential effect on the deductibles of five large insurers under this proposal.

Because this proposal was designed to significantly reduce potential industry losses, some insurers and industry participants we contacted said that it might make them more willing to offer coverage in areas affected by a future attack. As a result, supporters of the proposal argue that it would stabilize insurance markets in affected areas and facilitate rebuilding and recovery efforts. Moreover, the representative of one large insurer said that if the deductible was lowered to 5 percent, the insurer immediately would be willing to write more terrorism coverage, especially in downtown areas of larger cities. Since the insurer would be able to access the federal reimbursement at a lower level, the insurer's potential losses on its current book of business would be lower, thus freeing up additional capacity for terrorism coverage without having to purchase reinsurance from the private market to cover the additional risk.

Table 1. Current TRIA Deductibles of Five Large Insurers versus Deductibles Under a Recent Legislative Proposal

Dollars in billions			
	Direct written premiums	**Current TRIA deductible**	**Proposed TRIA deductible in case of attack**
Insurer A	24.8	4.9	1.2
Insurer B	14.6	2.9	0.732
Insurer C	14.4	2.8	0.721
Insurer D	12.7	2.5	0.635
Insurer E	7.5	1.5	0.375

Source: GAO analysis of Insurance Information Institute data.

Note: The legislative proposal—as outlined in S. 2621, 110th Cong. § 2 (2008) and H.R. 4721, 110th Cong. § 2 (2007)—would reset the TRIA deductible after a large terrorist attack where aggregate industry insured losses exceeded $1 billion.

While other insurers and industry participants we contacted were not necessarily opposed to this proposal, they remarked that its effects might be limited. As discussed previously, some large insurers already try to limit potential losses associated with a future terrorist attack to levels well below their current TRIA deductible of 20 percent of direct premiums. Therefore, it is not clear what effect lowering the TRIA deductible would have for such insurers in terms of the terrorism coverage that they are willing to offer. Second, as also discussed earlier, there may be significant market disruptions associated with another terrorist attack, which could limit coverage availability even if the federal government did assume greater liability for associated losses. For example, reinsurers, which are not subject to TRIA's requirements to make terrorism coverage available, again might limit the coverage they were willing to provide in the wake of another attack, which might limit the amount of coverage that primary insurers could offer. In addition, as happened following Hurricane Katrina, ratings agencies might increase the capital requirements or other standards insurers must follow to maintain and improve their ratings, potentially further limiting insurers' willingness to continue providing terrorism coverage in certain areas. Further, we note that lowering the TRIA deductible would increase the federal government's potential liability for terrorism-related losses.

Option 2: Permitting Insurers to Establish Tax-Deductible Reserves for Future Terrorism Losses

Another option would permit insurers to establish tax-deductible reserves, over a period of years, to cover the potential losses associated with future terrorist attacks. Under current federal tax law, insurers can take a deduction for losses that already have occurred and for setting aside reserves for fair and reasonable estimates of the amount the insurer will be required to pay on future losses. However, reserves for uncertain future losses are not currently tax deductible. Because the size and timing of terrorist attacks are uncertain, any reserves set aside for potential terrorism losses would be taxed as corporate income in the year in which they were set aside.[25]

We have reported previously that amending the tax code and permitting insurers to establish tax-deductible reserves could provide insurers with financial incentives to increase their capital and thereby expand their capacity to cover catastrophic risks, such as terrorism.[26] We also reported that supporters of this proposal argued that establishing such reserves would lower the costs associated with providing coverage and encourage insurers to charge lower premiums, which could increase coverage among policyholders. In addition, industry participants we interviewed said if insurers were able to establish tax-deductible reserves, a large terrorist attack could cause less of a strain or shock to industry surplus, or capital, which could help prevent insurer insolvencies in the wake of an attack.

However, several important challenges and tradeoffs may be associated with this option. For example, some industry participants we contacted said it would be difficult for insurers to determine the amount of funds to contribute to such a reserve each year because of the significant challenges associated with estimating the frequency of potential terrorist attacks. Without a reliable method for conducting such estimates, insurers would lack an analytical basis for reserving funds to cover potential losses.

Furthermore, we have reported that overall terrorism insurance capacity might not increase because insurers might use the reserves as a substitute for reinsurance that may have been purchased previously to manage the risks of potential terrorist attacks (reinsurance premiums are already tax-deductible).[27] Because reserving also would convey tax advantages, some insurers might feel that they could limit the expense of purchasing reinsurance. To the extent that insurers reduced their reinsurance coverage in favor of tax-deductible reserves, the industry's overall capacity would not necessarily increase. Insurers also might use the reserves to shield a portion of their existing capital (or retained earnings) from the corporate income tax or inappropriately use tax-deductible reserves to manage their financial statements by increasing the reserves during good economic times and decreasing them in bad times. Finally, we note that this proposal likely would reduce federal tax revenues.

Option 3: Forming a Group of Insurance Companies to Pool Assets for Terrorism Risks

Another proposal involves establishing a group of insurance companies to pool their assets, which may allow them to provide a greater amount of terrorism insurance coverage than could be provided by individual companies acting independently of one another. Insurance pools typically are formed to cover large risks, such as hurricanes, which traditional insurance markets do not address readily. For example, a pool could be created at the national level or state level; it could involve mandatory or voluntary participation from insurers; it could be prefunded or postfunded; and if losses exceed the reserves of the pool, the government could provide a financial guarantee or the pool could draw on some other method such as issuing bonds or borrowing funds to make up any shortfall. Table 2 shows that insurance pools have been established in Florida to cover hurricane risks and in the United Kingdom for terrorism risks.

Table 2. Examples of National and State Reinsurance Programs

Program	Program description	Coverage	Reinsurance or insurance	Government backstop	Voluntary or mandatory participation
Florida Hurricane Catastrophe Fund (FHCF)	The State of Florida created the FHCF after Hurricane Andrew. FHCF is a state-administered reinsurance program for insurers that offers residential property/casualty insurance in the state. Its purpose is to ensure reinsurance will remain available at relatively stable rates in the aftermath of hurricanes.	Residential property in case of hurricane in Florida	Reinsurance	None. FHCF may issue bonds, collect reimbursement premiums, or impose assessments on Florida insurance companies if funds are insufficient to meet obligations	Mandatory
Pool Reinsurance Company, Limited (Pool Re)	A mutual reinsurer in the United Kingdom that provides pooled industrywide reinsurance of terrorism risks after a specified industry retention level. Pool Re was formed in 1993 following reductions in reinsurance availability after terrorist bombings in London.	Commercial property, business interruption, and consequenti al losses for acts of terrorism	Reinsurance	Full government guarantee if pool resources are exhausted, after a 10 percent call upon insurers	Voluntary

Source: GAO analysis of information from Coalition to Insure Against Terrorism.

In addition to these programs, one large insurance broker, in consultation with several industry groups, has developed a proposal to form a $40 billion national reinsurance pool for commercial property terrorism risk.[28] Under this proposal, all insurance policies would cover losses from acts of terrorism and insurers would continue to charge policyholders their own rates for terrorism coverage in accordance with state laws. Insurers would purchase reinsurance coverage from the pool, which would determine its reinsurance premium rate based on analysis of a range of potential losses in urban, suburban, and rural areas. The claim reserves of the pool would be tax-exempt, allowing it to accumulate reserves tax-free from which to pay future losses. In the event of a certified terrorist attack, the insurance industry would pay 5 percent of losses and the pool would pay 95 percent of losses up to $40 billion. In the event the pool did not have the resources to pay its share of losses, the pool would be funded through the issuance of bonds.[29] The federal government would be responsible for losses in excess of $40 billion up to $100 billion. According to the plan, losses above $100 billion would be reviewed by Congress.

Some industry participants we contacted expressed general support of an insurer pool to enhance the availability of terrorism insurance coverage. For example, they said a pool could allow insurers to transfer a significant portion of their terrorism-related risk to an outside entity over time, and they could use the accumulated surplus in the pool to provide higher amounts of coverage in the future. Industry participants also noted that a national pool would spread out terrorism risk across a wider base of policyholders of varying risk levels than individual insurers could do alone and would allow insurers to better manage their total accumulations of terrorism risk.

However, several challenges and disadvantages also may be associated with this option. For example, as is the case with tax-deductible reserves, it may be difficult to develop a reliable basis for determining the appropriate size of the pool because of the inherent challenges in estimating the frequency of terrorist attacks. Moreover, other information suggests that insurance pools would not necessarily increase the industry's capacity or ability to offer additional terrorism insurance coverage. According to a study by a global consulting firm on a proposed workers'-compensation pool for terrorism risk and other industry participants, a reinsurance pool might not create new industry capacity or bring in additional capital to support writing more business.[30] The study notes that if the industry as a whole does not have enough capital to manage terrorism risk, then neither can an industry pool that simply combines existing industry capital in a new structure. Furthermore, we note that if premiums paid to the pool were tax deductible as are traditional reinsurance premiums, insurers simply might substitute pool reinsurance for traditional reinsurance, as might be the case with tax-deductible reserves for individual insurers. Finally, if the pool was a tax-exempt entity, tax-deductible reserves for an insurance pool could reduce federal revenues.

Option 4: Facilitating the Issuance of Onshore Catastrophe Bonds through Revisions to the Federal Tax Code

Another proposal is that the federal government establish certain tax advantages for catastrophe bonds, which supporters argue could facilitate their use for covering terrorist attacks.[31] Catastrophe bonds generally have been issued to cover natural events, such as earthquakes or hurricanes, rather than terrorist attacks and historically have been created in offshore jurisdictions where they are not subject to income or other tax. Under this proposal, tax treatment of catastrophe bonds would be similar to the treatment received by certain issuers of asset-backed securities, which generally are not subject to tax on the income from underlying assets that is passed on to investors.[32] We previously reported that the total costs of issuing catastrophe bonds—including transaction costs such as legal fees—significantly exceed the costs of traditional reinsurance, which may have limited the expansion of the market.[33] Facilitating the creation of onshore transactions by changing the tax code to encourage issuance of catastrophe bonds within the United States could reduce transaction costs.

Some insurance industry participants we contacted said that catastrophe bonds, by tapping into the securities markets, offered the opportunity to expand the pool of capital available to cover terrorism risk. They also said that amending the tax code to facilitate the bonds' issuance in the United States could be beneficial in achieving that goal. However, many industry participants said, consistent with findings in our previous reports, that the development of catastrophe bonds for terrorism risks involves significant challenges. These challenges may greatly exceed any benefit that would be derived from amending the tax code. As with other options discussed previously, the industry participants said that because of the difficulties associated with estimating the frequency of terrorist attacks, it would be very difficult to structure a catastrophe bond for terrorism that would be acceptable to investors. Data are available on the historical frequency and severity of natural events, such as hurricanes and earthquakes, which helps investors assess the risks that they face in purchasing catastrophe bonds for such risks. Without similar data for terrorist attacks, it is unlikely that a viable market for catastrophe bonds will be established regardless of revisions to the tax code that are designed to help ensure such an outcome. We also have previously reported that the federal government could lose tax revenue under this option and that the proposed changes to the tax code might create pressure from other industries for similar tax treatment.

Option 5: Revising Certain State Regulations and Insurance Coverage Requirements

Some industry participants have suggested that states could take certain actions to revise their insurance statutes or regulations to increase insurer capacity for terrorism risk, including amending rate regulation policies and laws on coverage requirements. While, according to information from NAIC, most state insurance regulators do not review rates for large commercial property/casualty insurance contracts, several insurance company representatives said that their ability to charge risk-based prices for terrorism coverage was constrained by insurance statutes and regulations in certain states and the prices these states approved did not reflect the risk to which the insurers were exposed.[34] Additionally, a few industry participants said that terrorism insurance availability may be limited in states that have adopted the Standard Fire Policy (SFP).[35] Under the SFP, property insurers are required to cover losses from fire regardless of the cause of the fire, including a terrorist attack, even if the policyholder declined terrorism coverage. Consequently, the industry participants said that the SFP influences the amount of property insurance that insurers provide, including terrorism insurance, and the premiums that they charge in states that have adopted it. Therefore, some insurers have suggested that states amend their SFP statutes so that insurers would not be responsible for fire losses resulting from terrorism.

While most states do not regulate prices for commercial property risks, where prices are regulated the state regulators are unlikely to disapprove insurers' rate requests because insurers are in a better position to judge the necessity of the price than the regulator, as long as the request is generally in line with current market prices, according to a representative from NAIC. In addition, other available information suggests that state actions on rate regulation or coverage requirements may have a limited effect on the availability of terrorism insurance coverage. As discussed in this chapter, some policyholders, particularly in Manhattan, may face initial challenges in obtaining terrorism coverage at prices viewed as reasonable. However, according to state regulatory officials, New York is one of the states that generally does not regulate premium rates for large commercial properties, so state regulation does not appear to be a significant factor in the city where insurance challenges appear to be most pronounced.[36] On the other hand, unlike several other states, New York and California have not revised the SFP to limit insurer liability resulting from the fires associated with terrorist attacks, according to information from industry analysts. While the SFP may therefore have an influence on the availability of terrorism insurance in such locations as Manhattan and San Francisco, it is difficult if not impossible to determine the influence as compared to other factors in these cities, particularly the potential losses associated with attacks on high-value buildings that may be in proximity to one another.

AGENCY COMMENTS

We provided a draft of this chapter to Department of the Treasury and NAIC for their review and comment. In oral comments, Treasury and NAIC officials said that the report was informative and useful. They also provided technical comments that were incorporated where appropriate.

Yvonne D. Jones
Director, Financial Markets and Community Investment

APPENDIX I: OBJECTIVES, SCOPE, AND METHODOLOGY

Our objectives were to describe (1) whether the availability of terrorism insurance for commercial properties is constrained in any geographic markets and the effect of any constraints on pricing and coverage amounts, (2) factors limiting insurers' willingness to provide coverage, and (3) advantages and disadvantages of some public policy options to increase the availability of property terrorism insurance.

To assess whether the availability of terrorism insurance for commercial properties is constrained in any geographic markets and the effect of any constraints on pricing and coverage amounts, we reviewed relevant literature and compiled and analyzed available data on insurance and reinsurance industry capacity, terrorism insurance take-up rates, and terrorism insurance pricing. We also interviewed representatives of more than 100 organizations with knowledge of the nationwide terrorism insurance market and with expertise in specific geographic markets. Entities with a national perspective included insurer and policyholder trade associations, individual policyholders, national insurance and reinsurance brokers, and insurance and reinsurance companies. We obtained information on specific geographic markets from state regulators, regional insurance brokers and insurance companies, and local property owners. The geographic markets we studied represent locations considered to be at high, moderate, and low risk of exposure to terrorist attacks—Atlanta, Boston, Chicago, New York, San Francisco, and Washington, D.C. We selected these markets based on rankings of locations by risk of terrorism exposure that accounts for the risk of terrorist attacks and the potential for associated losses from the Insurance Services Office, an insurance industry analytics firm. We spoke with representatives of policyholders that own hundreds of properties nationwide, including

- more than 200 properties in New York City,
- more than 100 properties in Washington, D.C.,
- at least 30 properties each in Chicago and San Francisco,
- about 30 properties in Boston and 60 in Atlanta, and

- numerous properties across the United States including major cities such as Los Angeles and Houston.

These properties included large office towers in major U.S. cities, properties in proximity to high-profile federal buildings, hotels, industrial buildings, hospitals, sports stadiums, and residential properties in locations throughout the United States. The policyholders also represented a variety of industries that included real estate, transportation, financial services, health, hospitality, and entertainment. In addition to one-on-one interviews, we also conducted group discussions with representatives of 14 policyholders at the annual Risk and Insurance Management Society conference in San Diego, California, in April 2008. Although we selected industry participants to provide broad representation of market conditions geographically and by industry, their responses may not necessarily be representative of the universe of insurers, insurance brokers, policyholders, and regulators. As a result, we could not generalize the results of our analysis to the entire national market for commercial property terrorism insurance. We determined that the selection of these sites and participants was appropriate for our objectives and that this selection would allow coverage of geographic areas, key markets, major insurers and policyholders, and other organizations related to terrorism insurance so as to generate valid and reliable evidence to support our work.

To identify the factors limiting insurers' willingness to provide terrorism insurance coverage, we selected large, national insurance companies to interview based on their market share in the states we studied. These national insurance companies held from 37 to 52 percent of the market share in the states we studied, according to information provided by the Insurance Information Institute. In addition, we interviewed representatives of regional insurance companies in our selected markets. We also spoke to representatives of seven reinsurance companies, including two of the largest worldwide reinsurance companies, risk modeling firms, state regulators, and two credit rating agencies. Although we selected insurers to provide broad representation of size and geographic scope, we could not generalize the results of our analysis to the entire population of commercial property insurers.

To explore the advantages and disadvantages of some public policy options to increase the availability of property terrorism insurance, we relied on our interviews with the industry participants described above. We also interviewed academics who have written on the topic of terrorism insurance, and representatives of research organizations and consumer interest groups. We selected the option that would reduce insurers' TRIA deductibles in areas affected by a future large terrorist attack from two recent legislative proposals. We selected the other options—allowing insurers to establish tax-deductible reserves, forming a group of insurance companies to pool assets, and facilitating the use of catastrophe bonds through changes in the tax code and amending state regulations or statutes—from literature we reviewed, our prior reports, and interviews we conducted with industry participants. The selected options were representative of the range of possible options. We did not attempt to evaluate the prospective effect of these options and, therefore, did not come to any conclusions about the advisability of implementing these options.

We conducted this audit in Atlanta, Georgia; Boston, Massachusetts; Chicago, Illinois; New York, New York; San Diego, California; San Francisco, California; and Washington, D.C., from January 2008 to September 2008, in accordance with generally accepted government auditing standards. Those standards require that we plan and perform the audit to obtain sufficient, appropriate evidence to provide a reasonable basis for our findings and conclusions based on our audit objectives. We believe that the evidence obtained provides a reasonable basis for our findings and conclusions based on our audit objectives.

GAO's Mission

The Government Accountability Office, the audit, evaluation, and investigative arm of Congress, exists to support Congress in meeting its constitutional responsibilities and to help improve the performance and accountability of the federal government for the American people. GAO examines the use of public funds; evaluates federal programs and policies; and provides analyses, recommendations, and other assistance to help Congress make informed oversight, policy, and funding decisions. GAO's commitment to good government is reflected in its core values of accountability, integrity, and reliability.

End Notes

[1] Department of the Treasury, Board of Governors of the Federal Reserve System, U.S. Securities and Exchange Commission, and Commodity Futures Trading Commission, *Terrorism Risk Insurance: Report of the President's Working Group on Financial Markets* (Washington, D.C., September 2006), 8.

[2] Pub. L. No. 107-297, 116 Stat. 2322 (Nov. 26, 2002).

[3] Department of the Treasury regulation codified at 31 C.F.R. § 50.5(d) defines direct earned premiums as a direct earned premium for all commercial property and casualty insurance issued by any insurer for insurance against all losses, including losses from an act of terrorism, occurring at locations within the United States, or on U.S. air carriers or U.S. flag vessels, or at the premises of any U.S. mission. The Department of the Treasury provided further clarification that direct earned premiums are "earned as reported to the NAIC in the Annual Statement in column 2 of Exhibit of Premiums and Losses (commonly known as Statutory Page 14)" and cover all risks, not only for risks from terrorism. The NAIC is the National Association of Insurance Commissioners, which is an organization representing state insurance regulators.

[4] *See* Terrorism Risk Insurance Extension Act of 2005, Pub. L. No. 109-144, 119 Stat. 2660 (Dec. 22, 2005) and Terrorism Risk Insurance Program Reauthorization Act of 2007, Pub. L. No. 110-160, 121 Stat. 1839 (Dec. 26, 2007).

[5] Under the 2007 statute that reauthorized TRIA coverage, GAO was required to report to Congress on similar objectives by June 23, 2008. *See* 15 U.S.C. § 6701 note (Terrorism Insurance Program § 108(g)(3)). To satisfy this mandate, we made presentations to the Committee on Financial Services of the House of Representatives and the Committee on Banking, Housing, and Urban Affairs of the U.S. Senate on June 20 and June 23, 2008, respectively. The presentation, GAO, *Initial Results on Terrorism Insurance Availability in Specific Geographic Markets*, GAO-08-919R (Washington, D.C.: July 11, 2008) is available on GAO's Web site at http://www.gao.gov. This chapter is based largely on our prior work. However, we added additional information and analysis, including information on two additional public policy options that were not discussed in our prior work.

[6] Reinsurance companies provide insurance to insurers.

[7] TRIA defines an "act of terrorism" as any act that is violent or dangerous to human life, property, or infrastructure and is certified as an act of terrorism by the Secretary of the Treasury, in concurrence with the Secretary of State, and the Attorney General of the United States, which has resulted in damage within the United States, or outside of the United States in the case of an air carrier or vessel (as defined for purposes of TRIA) or to the premises of a U.S. mission, and was committed by an individual or individuals, as part of an effort to coerce the civilian population of the United States or to influence the policy or affect the conduct of the U.S. government by coercion. Acts of war and losses that in the aggregate do not exceed $5,000,000 are specifically excluded. *See* 15 U.S.C. § 6701 note (Terrorism Insurance Program § 102(1)).

[8] 15 U.S.C. § 6701 note (Terrorism Insurance Program §§ 102(7)(F) and 103(e)(1)(A)).

[9] 15 U.S.C. § 6701 note (Terrorism Insurance Program § 103(e)).

[10] *See* 15 U.S.C. § 6701 note (Terrorism Insurance Program § 103(e)(2)(A)(ii)).

[11] Representatives of this broker noted that these data are limited because locations are typically recorded where the client is headquartered, not necessarily where the insured properties are located. For example, a company

headquartered in New York City would be included in New York even if the vast majority of the company's property holdings are located elsewhere.

[12] According to a national trade association representing lenders, commercial real estate lenders typically require that terrorism insurance be included as part of the mortgaged property's all-risk insurance policy and that property insurance, including terrorism coverage, is maintained for the property for the duration of the loan.

[13] According to a national insurer trade association, insurance policies are typically in force for a 1-year period. The process of putting an insurance contract out for bid or negotiating new terms and conditions of the contract can take several months.

[14] A stand-alone terrorism insurance policy limits coverage to losses from terrorist attacks, in contrast to an all-risk policy that would cover losses from multiple risks or perils.

[15] Captive insurance companies provide value to large corporations using them for terrorism coverage. Under TRIA, insurers required to participate in the program are defined as entities "licensed or admitted to engage in the business of providing primary or excess insurance in any state." See TRIA Section 102(6). Because captives are licensed and admitted by the states, just like traditional insurance companies, captives are "insurers" under TRIA and participate in the program. Captives receive compensation for insured losses under the program, enabling captive owners to transfer a significant portion—85 percent—of their terrorism exposure to the federal government for qualifying terrorist attacks, after paying a deductible. Captives also have direct access to the private reinsurance market, enabling captive owners to transfer a portion of their exposure to private insurers, according to a reinsurer and captive manager. Finally, policyholders can reduce their insurance costs by creating captive insurers and setting premium rates according to their own claims experience. However, there are significant costs to establishing and maintaining captive insurers, as well as the possibility of the parent company experiencing significant financial losses.

[16] Policyholders generally determine the amount of coverage to purchase based on lender requirements or the amount of losses that could result in a terrorist attack, which for some is the total replacement cost of the largest building in a portfolio.

[17] In a September 2004 letter interpreting its implementation of TRIA, the Department of the Treasury raised questions regarding the integrity of forming or utilizing captive insurers to only provide stand-alone, single-risk TRIA-only coverage for losses from acts of terrorism. In this letter, the department explained that it would continue to monitor developments in the market for terrorism risk insurance to determine if future rulemaking is needed to address the role of captives under TRIA. The letter stated that the Department of the Treasury has concerns about the possibility that captives may be used as a tool for avoiding the program's requirements and deductible because captives providing stand-alone terrorism coverage would be able to access reimbursements through TRIA at a much lower level than other insurers writing multiple lines of insurance. This is because the deductible is calculated on all lines of coverage written, not only coverage for terrorism. The department's letter is online at http://www.treas.gov/offices/domestic-finance/financial-institution/terrorism-insurance/pdf/0924_2.pdf.

[18] An insurer's surplus is the difference between its assets and liabilities, or the company's net worth. The surplus is the financial cushion that insurers can draw on in case of unexpectedly high policyholder claims.

[19] For terrorism insurance, primary insurers typically purchase reinsurance up to the difference between what the primary insurers are willing to lose in a terrorist attack and their TRIA deductibles as well as coverage for their 15 percent co-share under the program.

[20] GAO, *Terrorism Insurance: Implementation of the Terrorism Risk Insurance Act of 2002*, GAO-04-307 (Washington, D.C.: Apr. 23, 2004).

[21] According to a trade insurance association representative, the capacity of the global reinsurance market has increased significantly in recent years. The representative said that a wave of $20 billion in new capital entered Bermuda companies after the September 11 attacks. Similarly, a second wave of $43 billion in new capital entered the market after Hurricane Katrina.

[22] Congressional Budget Office, *Federal Reinsurance for Terrorism Risks: Issues in Reauthorization* (Washington, D.C., August 2007).

[23] See S. 2621, 110th Cong. § 2 (2008) and H.R. 4721, 110th Cong. § 2 (2007). The proposal would reset the TRIA deductible after a large terrorist attack where aggregate industry insured losses exceed $1 billion.

[24] The proposal also would increase the deductible by 0.5 percent in each subsequent year with no terrorist attack.

[25] A "property casualty company loss reserve" is an accounting entry, a liability on the balance sheet, for the amount of money the company expects to pay out in the future to cover indemnity payments that will come due on policies already written for losses that already have been incurred and the costs of dealing with the associated claims. Loss reserves do not reflect the pattern of future claims payments. Premium payment funds that cannot be put into loss reserves must be treated as underwriting profits.

[26] GAO, *Catastrophe Risk: U.S. and European Approaches to Insure Natural Catastrophe and Terrorism Risks*, GAO-05-199 (Washington, D.C.: Feb. 28, 2005).

[27] GAO-05-199.

[28] Aon, *Property Terrorism Update, TRIA in the Balance* (New York, N.Y.: October 2005).

[29] The plan specifies that the U.S. government would provide a contingent guarantee to buy bonds issued by the pool if bonds could not be sold in the open market due to a terrorist attack. The bonds would be repaid by assessments levied on all policies from covered lines during the life of the bonds. The bonds would be tax-exempt and have a maturity of up to 30 years.

[30] The Tillinghast and Reinsurance businesses of Towers Perrin, *Workers' Compensation Terrorism Reinsurance Pool Feasibility Study, Summary of Study Findings and Conclusions* (March 2004). The study was facilitated by the American Insurance Association and funded by 14 insurers that account for roughly 40 percent of the workers'-compensation market.

[31] Catastrophe bonds are risk-based securities that pay relatively high interest rates and provide insurance companies with a form of reinsurance to pay catastrophe losses. A catastrophe bond offering typically is made through an investment entity that may be sponsored by an insurance or reinsurance company. The investment entity issues bonds or debt securities for purchase by investors, thus spreading risk.

[32] Asset-backed securities, for example, are backed by loans or accounts receivable originated by banks, credit card companies, or other providers of credit. Certain issuers of these securities, Real Estate Mortgage Investment Conduits (REMIC), are generally not subject to federal income tax. Instead the income of the REMIC is taxable to the holders of interests in the REMIC. *See* 26 U.S.C. §§ 860A-860G; GAO, *Catastrophe Insurance Risks: The Role of Risk-Linked Securities and Factors Affecting Their Use,* GAO-02-941 (Washington, D.C.: Sept. 24, 2002).

[33] For additional information about catastrophe bonds and related tax issues, see GAO-02-941; *Catastrophe Insurance Risks: Status of Efforts to Securitize Natural Catastrophe and Terrorism Risk*, GAO-03-1033 (Washington, D.C.: Sept. 24, 2003); *Natural Disasters: Public Policy Options for Changing the Federal Role in Natural Catastrophe Insurance*, GAO-08-7 (Washington, D.C.: Nov. 26, 2007); and GAO-05-199.

[34] According to information provided by NAIC, the following 10 states and district require prior approval of commercial property rates: California, Hawaii, Iowa, Maryland, Michigan, New Mexico, New York, North Carolina, North Dakota, South Carolina, and Washington, D.C. While the State of Michigan has a prior approval law, an NAIC representative said that the Commissioner has exempted insurers from filing rates and forms for commercial lines insurance products. Some states, like New York, also have exceptions for large commercial risks, which are discussed in this chapter.

[35] According to information from the Insurance Information Institute and the Insurance Services Office (ISO), states that do not allow exclusions to the SFP for terrorism, thereby requiring coverage for fire following an act of terrorism, are California, Georgia, Hawaii, Iowa, Illinois, Maine, Massachusetts, Missouri, North Carolina, New Jersey, New York, Oregon, Rhode Island, Washington, West Virginia, and Wisconsin. The Virgin Islands also do not allow SFP exclusions for terrorism. Some of these states exempt the SFP requirements for the commercial inland marine line of business. Connecticut and Virginia enable an exclusion of fire following a certified act of terrorism. Fire coverage in both of these states would be required if TRIA expired.

[36] New York Insurance Department officials told us that large commercial property policies (above $100,000 in premium) as well as certain types of other risks can operate in what is called a "Free Trade Zone" in the state, where insurers have more discretion on determining the prices and terms of coverage they offer as long as they adhere to New York's statute that they are "neither excessive, inadequate, nor unfairly discriminatory." According to information from NAIC, several other states also have similar provisions exempting large commercial risks from rate regulation.

In: Terrorism Insurance
Editor: Miguel H. Palacios
ISBN: 978-1-60741-794-1

Chapter 5

TERRORISM INSURANCE: MEASURING AND PREDICTING LOSSES FROM UNCONVENTIONAL WEAPONS IS DIFFICULT, BUT SOME INDUSTRY EXPOSURE EXISTS

United States Government Accountability Office

WHY GAO DID THIS STUDY

Terrorists using unconventional weapons, also known as nuclear, biological, chemical, or radiological (NBCR) weapons, could cause devastating losses. The Terrorism Risk Insurance Act (TRIA) of 2002, as well as the extension passed in 2005, will cover losses from a certified act of terrorism, irrespective of the weapon used, if those types of losses are included in the coverage. Because of a lack of information about the willingness of insurers to cover NBCR risks and uncertainties about the extent to which these risks can be and are being insured by private insurers across various lines of insurance, GAO was asked to study these issues. This report discusses (1) commonly accepted principles of insurability and whether NBCR risks are measurable and predictable, and (2) whether private insurers currently are exposed to NBCR risks and the challenges they face in pricing such risks. GAO collected information from and met with some of the largest insurers in each line of insurance, associations representing a broader cross section of the industry and state insurance regulators.

GAO makes no recommendations in this report.

WHAT GAO FOUND

Insuring NBCR risks is distinctly different from insuring other risks because of the potential for catastrophic losses, a lack of understanding or knowledge about the long-term consequences, and a lack of historical experience with NBCR attacks in the United States.

Measuring and predicting NBCR risks present distinct challenges to insurers because the characteristics of the risks largely diverge from commonly accepted principles used in determining insurability. According to these common principles, when assessing insurability, the risk generally must (1) have past occurrences sufficient in number and homogeneous enough (invoking the "law of large numbers") to enable insurers to accurately predict future losses, (2) be definite and measurable in terms of dollar value, (3) occur by chance, and (4) not result in catastrophic losses for the insurer. While the condition of insurability or uninsurability is not an absolute, NBCR risks generally fail to meet most or all of these principles of an insurable risk. Indeed, insurance experts GAO interviewed said that the potential severity of NBCR risks alone could diminish the willingness of some insurers to insure NBCR risks.

Although NBCR risks may not fully satisfy the principles of insurability, there are enough variations in exposure across lines of insurance that some insurers or some lines of insurance may have no willingness to offer coverage for NBCR, while others may choose to offer coverage for some or all of the risks. For example, even with TRIA, property/casualty insurers generally have attempted to limit their exposure to NBCR risks by excluding nearly all NBCR events from coverage, both for commercial property/casualty and homeowners. According to industry representatives, property/casualty insurers believe they have excluded NBCR coverage by interpreting existing exclusions in their policies to apply to NBCR risks, but some of the exclusions could be challenged in courts. Unlike property/casualty insurers, however, workers' compensation, life, and health insurers are exposed to NBCR risks and generally have not excluded them from coverage for a variety of reasons. Specifically, workers' compensation insurers generally offer NBCR coverage because many states limit the exclusion of perils for workers' compensation. Conversely, while life and health insurers may not always be required to insure NBCR risks, they generally face other challenges in segregating and excluding NBCR risks. However, representatives of workers' compensation, life, and health insurers expressed concerns that the prices they currently charge may not cover their potential exposures to NBCR risks, sometimes because of regulatory limitations, and generally because of difficulties in measuring and pricing for NBCR losses. Given the challenges faced by insurers in providing coverage for, and pricing, NBCR risks, any purely market-driven expansion of coverage is highly unlikely in the foreseeable future.

September 25, 2006

The Honorable Michael G. Oxley
Chairman
Committee on Financial Services
House of Representatives
Dear Mr. Chairman:

When considering possible terrorist events, among the most potentially devastating would be those caused by terrorists using unconventional weapons, also known as nuclear, biological, chemical, or radiological (NBCR) weapons. Because of the potential for catastrophic losses from an NBCR attack, representatives of the insurance industry have voiced doubts about its ability to pay for such losses, and members of Congress have raised concerns about costs to the federal government and citizens from losses not covered by insurance. In response to the insurance industry's reluctance to cover terrorism risks generally, Congress enacted the Terrorism Risk Insurance Act (TRIA) of 2002 for the commercial property/casualty industry, which requires insurers to provide coverage for terrorism and provides a defined level of reimbursement for certain losses.[1] However, limited information suggests that even with this federal financial backstop, the insurance industry continues to be reluctant to provide insurance to cover NBCR risks.

In light of the continuing debate about TRIA, which is set to expire in 2007, the lack of information about the willingness of insurers to cover NBCR risks, and uncertainties about the extent to which these risks can be and are being insured by private insurers across various lines of insurance, you asked that we study the extent to which NBCR risks are measurable and insurable. This report discusses (1) commonly accepted principles of insurability and whether NBCR risks are measurable and predictable and (2) whether private insurers currently are exposed to NBCR risks and the challenges they face in pricing such risks.

To identify commonly accepted principles of insurability and whether NBCR risks are measurable and predictable, we reviewed standard insurance references to identify principles that insurers consider when evaluating the insurability of risks. We relied primarily on *Fundamentals of Risk and Insurance*.[2] To determine the insurability of NBCR risks, we compared information we collected about the market for and nature of NBCR terrorism risk to the principles. Moreover, we obtained information from a limited number of insurance industry representatives, as well as firms that specialize in modeling terrorism and other catastrophic events for insurers (modeling firms), to identify the amount and types of data available to predict future losses from NBCR terrorist attacks.[3] For comparison, we also obtained descriptions of data typically available to calculate losses for other catastrophic risks such as hurricanes. To assess whether private insurers were exposed to NBCR events and how they price for NBCR risks, we identified state requirements for coverage of NBCR events, lines of insurance where insurers cover NBCR damage of their own accord, and circumstances where coverage of NBCR events could be less clear. Specifically, we obtained documentation on state requirements from the National Association of Insurance Commissioners (NAIC) and visited two states and the District of Columbia, which contain localities that are considered to be at higher risk than others for a terrorist attack. To assess whether lines of insurance could be exposed to NBCR attacks, we reviewed government and industry studies to obtain broad estimates of the amount of NBCR coverage for commercial property/casualty insurance available on the market, but these studies had certain methodological limitations. We also interviewed at least two of the larger insurers in each of the major lines of insurance (commercial and personal property/casualty, workers' compensation, and individual and group life and health); commercial property/casualty and group life reinsurers (companies that provide insurance for insurers); and selected trade associations. Although we obtained information from a limited number of insurers, we selected the insurers based on their market share for each line of insurance nationwide and in states with localities considered to be at higher risk for terrorist attacks. The insurers we selected represented between 13 and 38 percent of the national market for each line of insurance. To determine circumstances under which coverage of NBCR events might be less clear, we interviewed insurers and identified examples of language relating to coverage in insurance contracts that could be contested. Finally, to determine if and why insurers would be willing to offer more coverage for NBCR events in the future, we interviewed representatives of insurers, insurance trade groups, policyholders, and academic experts.

We conducted our work in California, New Jersey, New York, Massachusetts, and Washington, D.C., from February 2006 through September 2006 in accordance with generally accepted government auditing standards.

RESULTS IN BRIEF

Insuring NBCR risks is distinctly different from insuring other risks because of the potential for catastrophic losses, a lack of understanding or knowledge about the long-term consequences, and a lack of historical experience with NBCR attacks in the United States. Measuring and predicting NBCR risks present distinct challenges to insurers because the characteristics of the risks largely diverge from commonly accepted principles used in determining insurability. According to these common principles, when assessing insurability, the risk generally must (1) have past occurrences sufficient in number and homogeneous enough (invoking the "law of large numbers") to enable insurers to accurately predict future losses, (2) be definite and measurable in terms of dollar value, (3) occur by chance, and (4) not result in catastrophic losses for the insurer. Although these principles of insurability generally underlie insurers' decisions about what risks to insure and at what price, experience with NBCR and other more common risks illustrate that insurability occurs along a continuum. That is, at one end are risks that satisfy all the principles and are most likely to be insured and at the other end are risks that satisfy none of the principles and are least likely to be insured. In general, NBCR risks largely fail to meet most or all of the principles of an insurable risk. Indeed, insurance experts we interviewed said that the potential severity of NBCR risks alone could diminish the willingness of some insurers to insure NBCR risks.

Although NBCR risks may not fully satisfy the principles of insurability, there are enough variations across lines of insurance that some insurers or some lines of insurance may have no willingness to offer coverage for NBCR, while others may choose to offer coverage for some or all of the risks. For example, even with TRIA, property/casualty insurers generally have attempted to limit their exposure to NBCR risks by excluding nearly all NBCR events from coverage, both for commercial property/casualty and homeowners. According to industry representatives, property/casualty insurers believe they have excluded NBCR coverage by interpreting existing exclusions in their policies to apply to NBCR risks, but some of the exclusions could be challenged in courts. However, unlike property/casualty insurers, workers' compensation, life, and health insurers are exposed to NBCR risks and generally have not excluded them from coverage for a variety of reasons. Specifically, workers' compensation insurers generally offer NBCR coverage because many states limit the exclusion of any peril for workers' compensation. Conversely, while life and health insurers may not always be required to insure NBCR risks, they generally face other challenges in segregating and excluding NBCR risks. Another reason that life and health insurers may be more willing to insure NBCR risks is that while the loss of life and health effects from an NBCR event may be damaging to some companies, large life and health insurers might be able to diversify their risks geographically and spread their losses over time. However, representatives of workers' compensation, life, and health insurers expressed concerns that the prices they currently charge may not cover their potential exposures to NBCR risks, sometimes because of regulatory limitations, and generally because of difficulties in measuring and pricing for NBCR losses. Given the challenges faced by insurers in providing coverage for, and pricing, NBCR risks, any purely market-driven expansion of coverage is highly unlikely in the foreseeable future.

BACKGROUND

The insurance industry offers many types of coverages intended to protect businesses as well as individuals. While the extent of regulation varies by state and by line of insurance, state insurance regulators oversee the provision of insurance; for example, states may approve the rates (prices) insurers may charge and require insurers to cover certain events. In order to ensure the availability of terrorism coverage after September 11, Congress enacted TRIA to temporarily provide some property/casualty insurers some reimbursement for insured losses, including workers' compensation losses, resulting from specific acts of terrorism.

Insurance can be grouped into three main types: property/casualty, life, and health. Property/casualty insurance includes several types of insurance. Commercial property/casualty insurers cover physical losses to property, business interruptions or loss of use of buildings due to property damage, and also legal liability related to the maintenance of the property and business operations. Workers' compensation insurance is considered a separate category of commercial property/casualty insurance, and the insurers provide employers protection against work-related disability and death. In addition, with certain exceptions, almost all employers are required to provide some form of workers' compensation insurance to cover employer liability for workers who are killed, injured, or disabled on the job from any cause.[4] Personal lines of property/casualty insurance include policies for homeowners and automobile coverage. Homeowners insurance provides coverage for physical losses to the home, its contents, and additional living expenses for the owner while the home is uninhabitable.

Life insurers sell either individual or group policies that provide benefits to designated survivors after the death of an insured. Health insurers cover medical expenses resulting from sickness and injury.

State Regulation of Insurance Companies

States have primary responsibility for regulating the insurance industry in the United States, and state insurance regulators coordinate their activities in part through NAIC. The degree of oversight of insurance varies by state and insurance type. In some lines of insurance, such as workers' compensation, insurers may file insurance policy forms with state regulators, who help determine the extent of coverage provided by a policy by approving the wording of policies, including the explicit exclusions of some perils. According to an NAIC representative, while practices vary by state, state regulators generally regulate prices for personal lines of insurance and workers' compensation policies but not for group life or commercial property/casualty policies. In most cases, state insurance regulators perform neither rate nor form review for commercial property/casualty insurance contracts because it is presumed that businesses have a better understanding of insurance contracts than the average personal lines consumer. However, reinsurers—companies that provide insurance to insurers—generally are not required to get state regulatory approval for the terms of coverage or the prices they charge.

NBCR Weapons Represent Many Methods of Attack

Terrorism attacks, particularly including those using NBCR weapons, could result in catastrophic losses. Each type of weapon—nuclear, biological, chemical, and radiological—represents different methods of attack. Further, many different agents can be used to carry out a biological, chemical, or radiological attack. See table 1 for general descriptions of each type of weapon and examples of available agents.

Table 1. Description of NBCR Weapons

	Weapon description	Examples of agents
Nuclear	A nuclear explosion would have immediate blast effects that would destroy buildings. The explosion also would produce high-energy radiation and extreme heat, and form a cloud from which highly lethal radioactive material would fall. The overall effect of the weapon would depend on the size of the weapon and how high above the ground the detonation occurred.	The explosion of the weapon, a bomb or missile, would be generated through nuclear fission of uranium or plutonium atoms, or nuclear fusion of hydrogen isotopes.
Biological	Biological attacks can involve two basic types of biological agents: contagious and noncontagious. With most biological agents, an attack may not be recognized immediately because the symptoms may be attributable to several causes or because the disease the agent causes has an incubation period.	Many different agents such as smallpox or anthrax, each with its own characteristics, could be used for biological attacks.
Chemical	Chemical attacks entail the dispersal of chemical vapors, aerosols, liquids, or solids and affect individuals through inhalation or exposure to eyes and skin. Chemical weapons act very quickly to kill or harm humans, often within a few seconds.	Many different agents such as sarin and hydrogen cyanide, each with its own characteristics, could be used for chemical attacks.
Radiological	A "dirty bomb" uses conventional explosives to disperse radioactive material across the immediate area, which could vary in size depending on the size of the explosive. The primary short-term exposure hazard to humans would be inhalation of radioactive material suspended in the dust and smoke from the explosion.	Different radioactive agents, including americium, cesium, and plutonium, could be used to create a dirty bomb.

Sources: RAND, GAO.

Notes: For weapon descriptions, see Rand Public Safety and Justice, *Individual Preparedness and Response to Chemical, Radiological, Nuclear, and Biological Terrorist Attacks* (Santa Monica, California: 2003). For examples of biological and chemical agents, see GAO, *Combating Terrorism: Need for Comprehensive Threat and Risk Assessments of Chemical and Biological Attacks*, GAO/NSIAD-99-163 (Washington, D.C.: Sept. 14, 1999). For examples of radiological agents that can be used in dirty bombs, see GAO, *Nuclear Security: DOE Needs Better Information to Guide Its Expanded Recovery of Sealed Radiological Sources*, GAO-05-967 (Washington, D.C.: Sept. 22, 2005).

The agents used to undertake NBCR attacks have differing characteristics and properties and would affect people and property in myriad ways. Of the four types of NBCR attacks, a nuclear bomb would be the most likely to result in fires of any consequence. The intense heat produced by the nuclear explosion and subsequent reactions could produce extensive fires located throughout the area of detonation. While the detonation of a dirty bomb (conventional explosives used to disperse radioactive material) could result in blast damage, the resulting fire damage likely would be confined to the immediate area. However, the detonation of both nuclear and dirty bombs would release radioactive materials, resulting in the need to decontaminate buildings and provide immediate healthcare. The distance these radioactive agents disperse from the original detonation site would depend on many factors, including the strength of the explosive and meteorological conditions. While the release of chemical and biological agents is significantly less likely to result in fires of any consequence, the agents also have the potential to contaminate buildings and make them unusable for long periods. These agents could be released within buildings or outdoors, with chemical agents more likely than biological agents to result in immediate harm to humans. All NBCR attacks, depending on size of the explosion or the quantity of the agent, have the potential to result in fatalities, injuries, or illness.

The Terrorism Risk Insurance Act Program

After the events of September 11, when certain coverage for terrorism events disappeared, Congress passed TRIA.[5] This law created a temporary program that effectively functions as reinsurance—for the commercial property/casualty and workers' compensation insurance industries only.[6] Under TRIA, the federal government would reimburse insurers in these lines for 90 percent of their losses, up to a specified level, after the insurers paid a deductible. The program also would cover losses caused by NBCR attacks, if insurers had included this coverage in an insurance policy. However, coverage of NBCR attacks, as with other terrorist attacks, would have to meet the program's criteria to trigger reimbursements.

TRIA requires certain insurers to "make available" coverage for terrorist events that the Secretary of the Treasury has certified as committed by individuals acting on behalf of a foreign person or interest.[7] Commercial property/casualty insurers must offer terrorism coverage to their policyholders, although they could impose an additional charge. Policyholders have the option of not purchasing the coverage and adding a terrorism exclusion to their policies. If policyholders chose to purchase the terrorism coverage for their property/casualty policies, insurers then could not add any additional exclusions or conditional language to the policies.

In December 2005, Congress extended many of the same provisions of the original statute in the Terrorism Risk Insurance Extension Act of 2005, but increased the required amount insurers would have to pay in the aftermath of a terrorist attack.[8] While deliberating the extension of TRIA, Congress considered whether to cover additional lines of coverage, such as group life insurance, and set a lower deductible that applied only to NBCR terrorist events. However, Congress did not enact these changes. The TRIA extension, which continues to apply only to the commercial property/casualty industry, is set to expire on December 31, 2007.

APPLYING COMMON PRINCIPLES FOR ASSESSING INSURABILITY PRESENTS CHALLENGES IN MEASURING AND PREDICTING NBCR RISKS

Several commonly accepted principles underlie insurers' ability to determine whether to offer coverage for a particular risk and at what price. Ultimately, the decision becomes a question of whether sufficient information exists for insurers to accurately estimate potential losses. According to standard insurance theory, four major principles contribute to the ability of insurers to estimate and cover future losses: the law of large numbers, measurability, fortuity, and the size of the potential losses.[9] However, measuring and predicting losses associated with NBCR risks can be particularly challenging for a number of reasons, including lack of experience with similar attacks, difficulty in predicting terrorists' intentions, and the potentially catastrophic losses that could result. Nevertheless, models have been developed that attempt to assist insurers in evaluating terrorist and NBCR risks. However, many insurers and other insurance experts continue to believe that there is an insufficient basis for estimating the probable frequency of terrorist attacks, including NBCR attacks.

Four principles generally underlie an insurance company's willingness to provide insurance for a particular risk or type of risk. Each contributes to the insurer's ability to measure and predict, with a reasonable degree of accuracy, the likely frequency of occurrence and the probable severity of losses that will result from each occurrence. In the ideal situation, when all these factors are satisfied, the insurer can add other expenses and profits to the expected losses and determine a price that is appropriate to the risk. Insurers may still decide to offer insurance for risks that deviate from the "ideal." However, as one or more of the factors vary from the ideal, the ability of the insurer to estimate future losses decreases, the risk increases, and the insurer's capital is more exposed to inadequate prices for the coverage that the insurer offers. These principles are

- *The law of large numbers must apply.* There must be a sufficiently large number of homogeneous units exposed to random losses, both historically and prospectively, to make the future losses reasonably predictable. This principle works best when there are large numbers of losses with similar characteristics spread across a large group. For example, an automobile insurer could analyze annual data on the frequency and severity (cost) of accidents and the characteristics of drivers (gender or age) involved in the accidents to predict expected losses for certain types of drivers, and thus set premiums adequate to cover these losses. The greater the experience with losses, the better the insurer would be able to estimate both the frequency and the severity of future losses, based on what happened in the past.

- *The loss must be definite and measurable.* The insurer must be capable of determining whether a loss has taken place, and setting a dollar value on the amount of the loss.

- *The loss must be fortuitous or accidental.* That is, the loss must result from chance and not be something that is certain to happen. To the extent that a future loss approaches certainty, an insurer would have to charge the full value of the loss plus an additional amount for the expenses incurred.

- *The loss must not be catastrophic.* That is, the losses should not affect a very large percentage of an insurance company's policyholders at the same time, for example, in a limited geographic area. Alternatively, a catastrophic loss is one that is extraordinarily large relative to the amount of exposure in an insurance pool.

When applied to NBCR terrorist risks, these principles can help explain why NBCR risks are so challenging for insurers. Most importantly, because so few NBCR attacks have occurred, the pool of experience in the United States is very limited, and the law of large numbers does not help insurers to measure and predict the frequency and severity of future losses.[10] One of the reasons many insurers we interviewed had concerns about insuring NBCR risks was the small number of historical events that could be used as a basis for predicting the future frequency and severity of these risks. However, several of the academic experts we interviewed also noted that a limited number of historical events did not automatically make a risk uninsurable.[11] For example, insurers have covered risks related to commercial satellites for which there has been a very limited record of losses; however, several of the experts noted that for commercial satellites the prospective loss is measurable and documentation is available to assess their safeguards.

In addition to the inapplicability of the law of large numbers, insurers also told us that they are not able to fully measure the costs of NBCR terrorist risks (that is, the potential severity). Because certain types of NBCR attacks could have long-term or uncertain consequences, insurers may not be able to measure, or even clearly identify, their prospective losses. Almost all of the insurers we interviewed indicated uncertainties about the scope of potential losses as a factor contributing to difficulties in insuring NBCR risks. For example, according to America's Health Insurance Plans (AHIP), a national trade association for health insurers, some NBCR attacks could produce latent illnesses such as cancer.[12] The costs to health insurers would not be immediate but would occur in the years to come. In addition, representatives of insurers and an insurance broker with knowledge of the property/casualty market told us that they believed the costs of some NBCR events would be uncertain because of difficulties in estimating how much time would pass before buildings were successfully decontaminated (for example, after an anthrax attack) or before anyone would even be willing to enter contaminated locations (for example, after a nuclear attack) to assess the damage, making the areas unusable for a long time.

Moreover, losses must be fortuitous or accidental. By definition terrorist events, including NBCR, are deliberate and do not occur by chance. As we previously reported, unlike storms and accidents, terrorism involves an adversary with deliberate intent to destroy, and the probabilities and consequences of a terrorist act are poorly understood and difficult to predict.[13] In other words, even if an extensive history of NBCR terrorism experiences existed, without the element of randomness, it would not necessarily be indicative of the future frequency and severity of terrorist events. Likewise, according to the American Academy of Actuaries and the Insurance Information Institute, predicting terrorist risks is particularly difficult because the attacks are not random; they are intentional, and the attack characteristics are not likely to be constant, as terrorists adjust their strategies.[14]

Finally, insurance experts told us that NBCR risks could represent the potential for catastrophic (severe) losses because of the concentration of risks that could face either a particular insurer or the industry. Most of the academic experts we interviewed stressed that the potential for catastrophic losses, rather than the lack of reliable data on the frequency and severity of NBCR risks, made insurers reluctant to insure them. Several of these experts observed that in Florida, where the risk of hurricanes is both greater and more predictable than NBCR terrorism risks, insurers were leaving the state because of their exposure to catastrophic losses, perhaps more so than the unpredictability of the risk. An NBCR event, like a natural catastrophe, could result in catastrophic losses if it created significant losses to a high proportion of insureds in a particular geographic area. Should these events take place in urban areas that serve as major places of employment, they could result in tremendous exposure for lines of insurance providing coverage for workers, such as health or workers' compensation.[15] In addition, as explained by representatives of the New York Department of Insurance, because NBCR risks have the ability to cut across many lines of insurance in a concentrated geographic area, large insurance companies that typically cover several lines of insurance could find it very difficult to diversify their risk portfolios. According to the American Academy of Actuaries, the prospect of catastrophic losses from an NBCR event could be far larger than insurers could sustain without impairing their ability to continue providing all other insurance coverages.[16]

The prospect of catastrophic risk poses additional problems because insurers, like most businesses, generally have two major objectives. First, they expect to make a profit for their owners. Second, they plan to survive so as to operate in the future. Several of the academic experts we interviewed questioned the incentive insurers would have to insure risks, such as catastrophic NBCR attacks, that might jeopardize their financial soundness and profitability. If an insurer were faced with the potential for a catastrophic loss—that is, one that threatened its solvency or its survival—the insurer would be less likely to be willing to provide insurance, or at a minimum, the insurer would limit its exposure to the extent that it could. The larger and more uncertain the estimates of projected losses, the less likely an insurer would be willing to voluntarily insure the risk. Moreover, insurers could have another disincentive to insuring catastrophic risks for which they might not be adequately capitalized—the prospect of receiving a low rating from a rating agency. We interviewed representatives from three rating agencies, two of whom said they generally viewed NBCR risks as not insurable because of their potential for catastrophic losses.[17] For example, a representative from one credit rating agency said that if his company considered existing potential exposure to NBCR risks when analyzing commercial property/casualty insurers, they might have to downgrade ratings due to the magnitude of potential losses.

Because the frequency and severity of NBCR risks are difficult to measure, insurers have turned to techniques and processes that they have applied to other catastrophic risks. As we previously reported, insurers have come to rely on computer models and modeling firms to assist them in estimating the frequency and severity of catastrophic events and the probable losses that they might face.[18] Since Hurricane Andrew in 1992, insurers have recognized the challenges associated with insuring low-frequency, high-cost risks such as natural disasters and increasingly have turned to the use of computer models to better estimate the expected frequency and severity of the risks. After September 11, the owners of these models developed them to estimate the effects of man-made, or terrorist, events as well. However, as noted by the Insurance Information Institute and other insurance experts, estimating the incidence of terrorism is fundamentally different and vastly more difficult than forecasting natural catastrophes, where insurers can learn much about the frequency and severity of events through historical claim data, meteorological and geological records, and increases in scientific knowledge.[19]

In view of the limited history of NBCR attacks in the United States, representatives of the modeling firms reported to us that they generally have relied on panels of terrorism experts to assess threats posed by terrorists. While these experts do not have access to current classified data, they use their judgment and expertise to assess the probability (that is, the future occurrence or frequency) of future terrorist attacks. For example, the experts assess the likelihood of terrorists targeting urban areas, based on population density and perceived importance, as well as well-known buildings within those areas. Moreover, the experts also consider the level of difficulty of using weapons of different sizes and capacities as a way of estimating the potential severity of terrorist attacks. The modeling firm representatives reported that they use a number of statistical techniques to convert the subjective opinions of their experts and the characteristics of NBCR weapons into quantified estimates of the frequency and severity of potential losses. While we did not assess the capabilities of these models, we have noted in a previous report that some federal agencies, even with access to classified data, have difficulty including in their risk assessments the relative probability of various terrorist threat scenarios.[20] Representatives of insurers and insurance brokers also said that they generally had little confidence in the ability of models to estimate the frequency of future terrorist attacks, and the American Academy of Actuaries noted that while there has been some development of terrorism models since September 11, quantification of terrorism exposure still was extremely difficult.[21] The Academy also noted that the probabilities associated with the occurrence of a terrorist attack have remained somewhat judgmental and a key source of uncertainty.

Representatives of insurers told us that the models can be useful in simulating scenarios for particular NBCR attacks in specified locations, allowing them to estimate the potential severity of possible losses for specific events. Using available engineering, scientific, and demographic research, the models can estimate insured potential losses for the portfolios of individual insurers. Several insurers and brokers said that they found models, including those that they may have created themselves, useful in managing insurers' exposure to terrorism risks.

Finally, insurance experts and representatives of insurers and reinsurers we interviewed agreed that difficulties in predicting NBCR events, as well as the prospect for catastrophic losses, make these risks difficult to insure.[22] However, as noted by several of the experts from academia, even though a risk may not satisfy all the principles of insurability, insureds may be able to find some amount of coverage. Several experts noted that insurability is not simply an issue of extremes—that is, either insurable or uninsurable. Rather, as specifically noted by one, the insurability of events should be viewed as a continuum, with some events such as NBCR being on the extreme end of the continuum.

Insurers' Exposure to NBCR Risks Varies Widely by Line of Insurance, and Insurers Offering Coverage Face Challenges in Pricing

Insurers' exposure to NBCR risks varies widely by line of insurance, and insurers offering coverage face challenges in pricing. In view of the underlying difficulties in insuring NBCR risks, property/casualty insurers generally have tried to exclude such events from their coverage. However, for reasons that vary somewhat by line of insurance, workers' compensation, life, and health insurers generally offer coverage for NBCR events. Insurance industry representatives told us that most property/casualty insurers have used long-standing policy exclusions to limit coverage of NBCR events, although experience with these types of exclusions suggests that they could be challenged in court. Representatives of property/casualty insurers said that these risks continue to be unattractive to insure because of difficulties in predicting the frequency and severity of these risks, the potential for large and uncertain losses, and the limited amount of private reinsurance. Despite similar concerns and subsequent difficulties in setting prices due to lack of reliable historical data, coverage for workers' compensation, life, and health insurance generally is available on the market. In large part, insurers provide this coverage, particularly workers' compensation, because they are required to by states, or because the coverage (for example, life insurance) does not readily lend itself to excluding one type of risk. Nevertheless, insurance and state regulatory officials expressed particular concerns about whether the prices set for workers' compensation insurance would cover potential losses, should a major NBCR event occur. Representatives of life and health insurers told us that generally their prices did not reflect their potential exposure to NBCR risks.

Relatively Little NBCR Coverage Available in Property/Casualty Market Because Most Insurers Remain Unwilling to Cover Risks

Unlike workers' compensation, life, and health insurers, insurers selling property/casualty insurance largely have excluded NBCR risks from their policies. Since Congress passed TRIA, the supply of commercial property/casualty insurance for conventional terrorism appears to have increased, yet insurance policies covering NBCR risks have remained in short supply. In its most recent survey of terrorism insurance in the commercial property/casualty industry, Treasury found that the percentage of insurers that reported that they wrote some coverage for terrorism using conventional weapons (that is, not NBCR) increased from 73 percent in 2002 to 91 percent in 2003 and 2004.[23] In contrast, the percentage of insurers that reported covering NBCR risks in some of their policies remained about the same during that general period and was significantly smaller—about 35 percent.[24] Moreover, as explained by Treasury officials, the 35 percent represented insurers that offered any kind of coverage for NBCR risks, meaning that an insurer would be counted as offering NBCR coverage even if it offered only one policy for one type of NBCR risk.

Representatives of insurance and insurance brokerage companies also told us there was a very limited supply of NBCR coverage in the commercial property/casualty marketplace. Representatives of the three largest brokerage firms that find property/casualty insurance coverage for large commercial businesses told us that insurers offering terrorism coverage exclude NBCR risks. According to representatives of insurers, exclusions for NBCR risks are contained in policies offered by commercial property/casualty insurers underwriting in regulated insurance markets and also are contained in stand-alone terrorism insurance policies offered by specialty insurers in the nonregulated market.[25] A representative of one of the specialty insurers with whom we spoke said the company offered very limited amounts of NBCR coverage, typically for one or two of the risks. For example, this company would offer $10 million of biological and chemical coverage for certain commercial properties, but the insurer would not provide coverage above that threshold.

Representatives of insurance and insurance brokerage companies we interviewed said that even though TRIA would cover NBCR losses incurred by an insurer the same as it would any other covered terrorist losses, little coverage for NBCR risks was available because commercial property/casualty carriers largely viewed NBCR risks as uninsurable. According to representatives of two large commercial property/casualty insurers, both of whom underwrote insurance in states with localities considered at higher risk for a terrorist attack, the current structure of TRIA offered little incentive to cover NBCR losses, even though TRIA would provide coverage for some insured NBCR events. For example, they said that because their companies offered workers' compensation insurance in areas at higher risk for terrorism, the companies were less likely to increase their level of exposure to NBCR events by also offering NBCR coverage in their commercial property and general liability policies.[26] Under TRIA, the more business an insurer writes, the larger its deductible; and the more lines of insurance an insurer writes, the more it is exposed to losses from a catastrophic event.[27] In addition, because of uncertainties surrounding the frequency and severity of NBCR events as well as the enormity of potential losses, representatives of insurers we interviewed said that they would have difficulty setting prices to cover such losses, even using information from the modeling firms. These representatives also expressed concerns about the potential insured losses of an NBCR event being largely undeterminable for many years after the event occurred. Such an event could have many long-term consequences—for example, the extent and duration of remediation for a contaminated zbuilding, the resulting business interruption to the policyholder, and any related litigation involved.[28] Finally, as confirmed by representatives of the Reinsurance Association of America, private reinsurance—the risk-spreading mechanism that insurers typically use to reduce their potential losses—provided very limited amounts of coverage for NBCR risks in the property/casualty market.

Although Property/Casualty Insurers Remove Coverage for NBCR Events through Exclusions, They Could Be Challenged

Property/casualty insurers long have sought to limit their exposure to certain perils, such as flood, that they consider uninsurable. Property/casualty insurers have written exclusions related to nuclear hazard risk into their standard policies for decades, generally to protect themselves from losses related to nuclear power plant accidents. Representatives of insurance companies and brokerage firms agreed that existing nuclear hazard exclusions were broad enough to likely exclude any losses resulting from nuclear and radiological events, including a terrorist attack.[29]

According to these same insurance industry representatives, property/casualty insurance contracts issued prior to September 11 did not specifically include references to losses from the terrorist release of biological and chemical agents.[30] Rather, Insurance Services Office

(ISO) officials told us that the standard contracts they provided for industry use contained language that excluded coverage for losses caused by pollution and contamination. For instance, the pollution exclusion was developed to exclude coverage for the release of many different types of substances— from asbestos to pesticides—that could cause harm to people and the environment. Representatives of some of the insurers we interviewed believed that their pollution and contamination exclusions also might allow property/casualty insurers to exclude losses caused by biological and chemical agents released by a terrorist. However, representatives of one insurance broker we interviewed suggested that pollution and contamination exclusions could be challenged in the courts if a biological or chemical event were to occur. Courts determine whether a particular substance is or is not a pollutant based upon, among other things, the language in the policy, the facts and circumstances of the case, and the law of the jurisdiction. As a result, the language of the standard pollution exclusion might be susceptible to broad interpretation by the courts. In other words, some uncertainty exists, even in the insurance industry, about how effectively the pollution and contamination exclusions would protect insurers against losses from a NBCR terrorist attack.

In addition to disputes over the exclusion of NBCR risks in policies, there are other situations where the extent of property/casualty insurers' coverage of such events could depend on judicial or other determinations.

- *Cause of loss.* According to standard nuclear exclusions, commercial policies would not cover damage caused by a nuclear blast. However, regardless of any exclusions, according to information provided by NAIC, approximately 16 states (including New York) require property/casualty insurers to cover losses from a "fire following" an event, irrespective of the cause of fire.[31] A national security expert told us that in the case of a nuclear bomb detonation, once the property was destroyed, insurers could dispute the extent to which fire (covered in fire following states) or the blast (excluded by the nuclear exclusion) caused the damage. In other contexts, disputes over the cause of loss often have been litigated. For example, many homeowners who suffered losses in Hurricane Katrina have filed lawsuits challenging property/casualty insurers' determinations about the cause of their losses.[32]

- *Certified as a terrorist act.* The Congressional Budget Office (CBO) has suggested that some NBCR events might not be readily identified as terrorist acts, as defined by TRIA, and therefore coverage—both for insurers and for their policyholders—would be unclear.[33] For example, the persons or person who in 2001 mailed letters contaminated with anthrax that killed several people and sickened many more remain(s) unknown.[34] However, should TRIA not be renewed in 2007, this particular determination would not apply.

In addition, homeowners' insurers, part of the personal property/casualty market, have long-standing exclusions in their policies, similar to the exclusions contained in commercial property/casualty policies. According to representatives of two large homeowners' insurers, the exclusions limited their exposure to NBCR risks. While these representatives also told us they have not excluded conventional terrorist events from their policies, they said their companies generally manage their exposure to any terrorism risks by diversifying their portfolios.

Demand for NBCR Coverage in Property/Casualty Market Is Difficult to Determine

The 2005 Treasury study reported that less than 3 percent of policyholders from a range of industries reported purchasing NBCR coverage in their commercial property/casualty insurance policies.[35] Further, although purchase rates for NBCR insurance do not necessarily reflect overall demand, a major reason for not purchasing NBCR insurance given by the survey respondents was that they did not believe they were at risk for an NBCR event. While the Treasury study did not break down purchase rates for NBCR insurance by industry sector, another study of the market for terrorism insurance conducted by insurance brokers found that companies in the real estate, financial, and health care sectors had the highest rates for purchasing terrorism insurance.[36] Although the brokerage firm study does not specifically address the demand for NBCR insurance, we consider demand for terrorism insurance generally to be a reasonable approximation of where demand for NBCR insurance might exist. For instance, demand for terrorism insurance may be strong in the real estate sector because terrorism coverage typically is required as part of a commercial business loan transaction, according to the Mortgage Bankers Association. However, representatives of the Mortgage Bankers Association also said lenders generally do not require NBCR coverage, because little or no coverage is available. In addition, a few of the academic experts we interviewed suggested that some individuals and businesses might not purchase NBCR coverage under the assumption that the federal government would cover losses from an NBCR attack, as the government agreed to do for some personal and commercial property losses resulting from Hurricane Katrina.

However, several risk managers we interviewed from the hospitality and transportation industries, as well as commercial property owners, all reported a willingness to buy NBCR coverage in the private market. These managers expressed frustration at not being able to purchase insurance for NBCR risks, which they said they could do little to prevent or mitigate, particularly because an NBCR attack would be an intentional act. One of the risk managers that we interviewed noted that his company could not find enough NBCR coverage for even one building, so the company used a captive to self-insure against NBCR risks.[37]

Insurers in Workers' Compensation, Life, and Health Generally Cover NBCR Risks, but Prices May Not Take Account of Potential Losses

Should an NBCR event occur, workers' compensation, life, and health insurers would be responsible for covering loss of life and medical treatment for injuries because they generally provide coverage for these events. Following September 11, NAIC issued guidance stating its member state regulators believed terrorism exclusions were "not necessary" or were "inappropriate" for workers' compensation, life, and health insurance policies, with exceptions limited to cases where insurers could demonstrate they would become insolvent from offering the coverage.[38] According to an NAIC representative, regulators did not perceive exclusions as necessary because they presumed these insurers were diversifying their risks in these lines by insuring individuals across the country.

Workers' Compensation Insurance Generally Covers All Perils, Including NBCR Risks, but Pricing Challenges Exist

Workers' compensation insurers must cover losses from NBCR events that occur at the workplace, including related illnesses and injuries. According to multiple sources, applicable state laws generally require workers' compensation insurers to cover nearly all perils, including those from NBCR risks.[39] In addition, according to representatives of the National Council on Compensation Insurance (NCCI), an organization that prepares insurance rate (price) recommendations for workers' compensation, under state workers' compensation laws, employers are responsible for covering unlimited medical costs and a portion of lost earnings for injuries or illnesses that occur during the course of employment, regardless of the cause.[40]

While workers' compensation insurers generally are not permitted to exclude any perils from coverage, insurer representatives advised us that any surcharges they may be permitted to charge for NBCR exposure likely would not cover potential losses. According to NCCI representatives, recognizing that workers' compensation insurers have exposure to terrorism losses, at least 36 states, including the District of Columbia, have allowed workers' compensation insurers to file rates that include an additional surcharge (an average of 2 cents per $100 of employee payroll) for terrorism risk.[41] NCCI developed this statewide surcharge based on the results of a model, as a way for insurers that underwrite in states that belong to NCCI to cover potential losses from terrorism, including those from NBCR weapons. While representatives of NCCI were reasonably satisfied that the surcharges were actuarially sound, in the District of Columbia—where insurers may file the NCCI-developed terrorism surcharge—regulators did not believe that the surcharge was actuarially sound because of assumptions made in the model about localities designated to be at higher risk for terrorist events. Moreover, the willingness of state regulators that do not participate in NCCI to approve terrorism surcharges in workers' compensation may vary. For example, we obtained information from two large states that do not participate in NCCI and have geographic areas considered at higher risk for terrorism—New York and California. In New York, regulators have allowed workers' compensation insurers to file an additional surcharge for terrorism. However, representatives of the New York Compensation Insurance Rating Board (Rating Board) told us that the terrorism surcharge the Rating Board developed does not distinguish between conventional and NBCR risks.[42] They did not believe that the Rating Board could justify a higher surcharge to cover NBCR risks because of the limited historical data on NBCR attacks and further, if the Rating Board did, the cost would be so high that businesses would probably find it unaffordable. In contrast, California regulators have not permitted insurers to file rates with additional surcharges specifically for terrorism, including NBCR risks. California regulatory officials told us that they would reject any terrorist or NBCR risk surcharges because they thought such rate justifications were not based on recognized actuarial methods.[43]

Representatives of workers' compensation insurers we interviewed said that factors unique to workers' compensation also made it difficult for them to cover NBCR risks. First, as they explained, unlike some other lines of insurance, workers' compensation insurance covers losses beyond the expiration date of the policy. The representatives told us their most expensive claims typically came from workers who were disabled from illness or injury because they were entitled to lost wages as well as medical expenses. For NBCR events, quantifying medical expenses could be especially challenging because some illnesses or disabilities might not manifest until much later or could be difficult to trace to a workplace occurrence.[44] For example, representatives of workers' compensation insurers told us that in the case of smallpox, it might be difficult to determine whether the worker contracted the illness at work or elsewhere.[45] In addition, these representatives told us that they may be further constrained in their ability to adjust their price for specific geographic risks. Representatives of NCCI told us that terrorism surcharges must be applied equally throughout a state, thus the terrorism surcharge did not reflect that employers in certain areas, such as urban areas where employees might be more concentrated, had a greater exposure to terrorist events.[46]

Despite the exposure of workers' compensation insurers to NBCR risks, representatives of private market insurers and two public insurance funds told us that the availability of private reinsurance for these risks was limited.[47] Therefore, they explained that they largely would rely on TRIA to cover NBCR risks. As representatives of the private insurers explained, many of their private-market reinsurance policies specifically excluded NBCR risks, or to the extent coverage was available, reinsurers offered it at prices they could not afford. Representatives of the New York State Insurance Fund told us that they had not purchased reinsurance because they viewed the high costs of reinsurance for their market as unaffordable. As a result, should a large NBCR attack occur, these representatives said that their fund might have to turn to the state to help pay claims. In contrast, representatives of the California State Compensation Insurance Fund said that they were willing to pay higher prices based on available capacity for reinsurance for NBCR risks.

According to Life Insurers, They Generally Cannot Exclude Terrorism Coverage Including NBCR Risks

The American Council of Life Insurers officials, as well as representatives of life insurers we interviewed, told us they believed that most states do not allow for terrorism or NBCR exclusions in life insurance policies.[48] In two of the states specifically included in our review—New York and California—state insurance law and implementing regulatory policy prohibited both individual and group life insurance policies from excluding NBCR or other terrorism events.[49] On the other hand, regulatory officials from the third jurisdiction we included in our review, the District of Columbia, told us that they did not have any legal requirements that life insurers cover NBCR events and that several group life insurers recently filed policies with exclusions for NBCR risks.

While group life insurers have exposure to NBCR risks, representatives of group life insurers that provide coverage nationwide told us that charging higher rates to insureds at potentially greater risk for an NBCR event would be difficult. This is because of the way the insurers typically price coverage and their inability to determine which employers would be at greater risk for an NBCR event. Life insurers price their products based on mortality tables derived from experience with prior insurance contracts and calibrated for the effects of certain individual characteristics such as a smoking habit, or group characteristics such as occupation type. However, representatives of life insurers said that these tables do not take into account a greater number of deaths that could occur as a result of a terrorist or NBCR act.[50] Furthermore, these representatives told us that they have difficulty determining whether a particular employer or group would be more or less at risk for death from an NBCR event because they traditionally have not tracked the geographic locations of individuals covered by their policies.

However, whether losses from a large NBCR attack would be catastrophic for life insurers was unclear and could depend on the extent to which their portfolios were diversified. Representatives of national life insurers told us that they have a broad portfolio of exposure nationwide, which helps them diversify their risks. In the event of a large NBCR attack in which up to one million insured people died, representatives of the American Council of Life Insurers told us that most large life insurers probably would be able to pay the death claims. However, these representatives also said that small or medium-size group life insurers that received a significantly high number of death claims following an NBCR attack might be unable to pay claims and become insolvent, and that state guarantee funds would have to levy an assessment on the remaining insurers in the states to pay the claims.[51] Notwithstanding their belief that they could survive an NBCR attack, representatives of the two national insurers we interviewed were concerned about the companies' exposure to catastrophic NBCR losses. These representatives particularly were concerned because their companies generally insure all the employees of a given company. These employees could be concentrated in one geographic location, and the insurance companies could be liable for huge losses if an NBCR event led to widespread casualties in one area.[52]

In addition, life insurers do not have access to TRIA. Representatives of two group life insurers we interviewed said that their companies either had not found reinsurance for NBCR risks or the costs were very high relative to the amount of insurance that could be purchased. We also spoke with representatives of a large group life reinsurer who said their company provided some coverage for NBCR events, although the company limited this exposure to $100 million per event.

According to Health Insurers, They Face Unique Challenges in Determining Exposure to NBCR Risks

Although many health insurers cover groups of individuals concentrated geographically, representatives of AHIP and two national group health insurers told us that determining overall exposure to NBCR risks was challenging. Further, they explained that state regulation of NBCR coverage was not the primary reason they covered terrorism risks, and AHIP could not provide us documentation of regulatory requirements for NBCR coverage. Nevertheless, insurance regulatory officials from two states with localities at higher exposure to terrorism risks—California and New York—told us they have not allowed health insurance policies to exclude medical expenses related to illness or injury sustained from an NBCR event.[53] In contrast, regulatory officials in the District of Columbia told us that they did not have any requirements that health insurers cover NBCR events.

Representatives of two national group health insurers we interviewed described the difficulties they would have in attempting to set actuarially sound prices for health risks from NBCR terrorist events. First, representatives of health insurers said that they typically price health coverage based on experience with their insured populations and without knowing the likely impact of NBCR risks, they could not develop actuarially sound prices for such a risk. Further, the representatives explained they tend to limit policy coverage by procedure or by individual, rather than by the source of the illness. For example, a representative of one health insurer told us that while the company did develop prices for other low-frequency, high-cost claims such as liver transplants, they could only do so because of prior experiences. Second, uncertainties over the long-term health effects of NBCR attacks, such as the need for psychological counseling or cancer treatment, make it difficult for insurers either to exclude

NBCR attacks from their coverage or charge additional prices for their coverage. A report from the American Academy of Actuaries, as well as representatives from AHIP, noted that harm from NBCR events could be widespread and persist for years, and in the years subsequent to the attack, it would be difficult to identify the source of the illness.[54] According to representatives of one insurer, this also would make direct attribution of an expense to an NBCR attack difficult.[55] Further, these representatives said that the ultimate costs of medical treatment would be unknown, as some factors such as whether hospitals would remain open and sufficient vaccines would be available, were controlled by local public health responders.[56] Finally, similar to life insurance, representatives of one health insurer told us they often lack information about the specific geographic locations of their insured populations, further limiting their ability to conduct risk-based pricing for events such as NBCR attacks.

Representatives of the health insurance industry told us private reinsurance for their coverage of catastrophic events generally was very limited. AHIP representatives told us that catastrophic reinsurance for health insurers was in short supply, expensive, and generally focused on covering large costs incurred by individuals, rather than large costs incurred by groups of individuals potentially exposed to the same risks. Representatives from health insurers also said that reinsurance was costly, but they had not specifically sought out coverage for NBCR risks. As is the case for life insurers, health insurers do not have access to TRIA.

As agreed with your office, unless you publicly announce the contents of this report earlier, we plan no further distribution until 30 days from the report date. At that time, we will send copies to the Ranking Minority Member of the House Financial Services Committee, other interested members of Congress, and NAIC. We also will make copies available to others upon request. In addition, this report will be available at no charge on GAO's Web site at http://www.gao.gov.

If you or your staff have any questions on this report, please contact me at 202-512-8678 or williamso@gao.gov. Contact points for our Offices of Congressional Relations and Public Affairs may be found on the last page of this report. GAO staff who made major contributions to this report are listed in appendix II.

Sincerely yours,

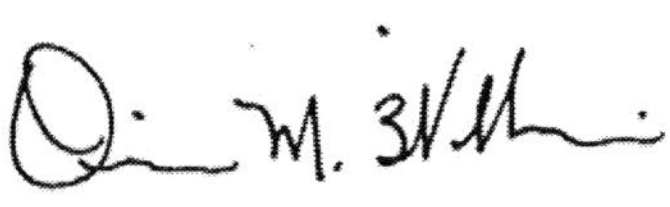

Orice M. Williams
Director, Financial Markets and Community Investment

APPENDIX I: OBJECTIVES, SCOPE, AND METHODOLOGY

Our objectives were to discuss (1) commonly accepted principles of insurability and whether nuclear, biological, chemical, and radiological (NBCR) risks are measurable and predictable and (2) whether private insurers currently are exposed to NBCR risks and the challenges they face in pricing such risks. As part of our review, we conducted interviews in California, New Jersey, New York, Massachusetts, and Washington, D.C. We conducted our review from February 2006 through September 2006 in accordance with generally accepted government auditing standards.

Principles of Insurability and Assessing Whether NBCR Risks Are Measurable and Predictable

To identify commonly accepted principles of insurability and whether NBCR risks are measurable and predictable, we reviewed standard insurance references to identify principles that underlie insurers' evaluations of the insurability of risks. We primarily relied upon *Fundamentals of Risk and Insurance,* but consulted additional references for consistency of explanation.[57] To determine the insurability of NBCR risks, we applied these principles based on information we collected about the market for, and nature of, NBCR terrorism risks. To enhance our understanding of the market for NBCR insurance, and factors that insurers might consider when deciding whether to offer this insurance, we consulted insurance experts, including the American Academy of Actuaries, the Insurance Information Institute, and insurance experts from academia, and a crosssection of insurers representing different lines of insurance.

Moreover, we obtained information about how NBCR terrorist risks are measured and predicted from three firms that specialize in modeling terrorism and other catastrophic events for insurers (modeling firms).[58] We chose these three firms because they are among the best known in the insurance industry. Representatives of these firms provided us with and identified the types of information they incorporate into their computer models, the methods that they use to estimate the potential frequency and severity of terrorist attacks with NBCR weapons, and the reasons they believe their products are of assistance to the insurance industry. We did not evaluate the ability of the models to predict the frequency and severity of NBCR or other catastrophic risks. For additional perspective, we also obtained descriptions of the types of data available to model insured losses from natural disasters, such as hurricanes, from a modeling firm and presentations made at a catastrophe modeling conference.[59]

Finally, to obtain a broad understanding of the characteristics of NBCR weapons and the types of damage they could cause, we consulted several sources of information. We interviewed representatives from RAND, a nonprofit research organization with a focus on national security issues, and reviewed RAND publications. In addition, we interviewed representatives of the U.S. Department of Homeland Security and reviewed reports. In addition, to identify the characteristics of biological, chemical, and radiological weapons, we used information from our own reports.

Assessing Exposure to NBCR Risks

To assess whether insurers are exposed to NBCR events, we identified lines of insurance that could be affected in the event of an NBCR terrorist attack: life, health, workers' compensation, commercial property/casualty, and homeowners insurance. Our information about insurer exposure in each of these lines came from multiple sources.

For an overview of the market nationwide, we interviewed representatives of three of the largest commercial insurance brokers and national insurance trade organizations—the American Council of Life Insurers, representing life insurers; America's Health Insurance Plans, representing health insurers; the Property Casualty Insurance Association of America, representing property/casualty insurers; the Reinsurance Association of America, representing reinsurance companies; and the Association of Bermuda Insurers and Reinsurers, representing off-shore specialty insurers and reinsurers. In addition, we interviewed representatives from Independent Insurance Agents and Brokers of America, an association of independent insurance agents and insurance brokers nationwide. Information from these trade associations helped provide a broader context for information we obtained from individual insurers and reinsurers and gave us some perspective on exposure for small and medium-sized insurers, insurers that we did not interview.

To obtain information on specific insurers' exposure to NBCR risks, we interviewed knowledgeable representatives of a total of 12 insurers, writing either one or several lines of insurance addressed by our study. Although the time frames of our report only permitted us to obtain information from selected insurers, we believe that these insurers were knowledgeable based on their broad exposure for their respective lines of insurance nationwide and their knowledge of markets at higher risk for terrorism. To select insurers to interview, we obtained 2004 market share data based on direct written premiums from the Insurance Information Institute and Moody's, the most recent available data at the time of our review.[60]

Seven of the insurers we interviewed that provide coverage in the property/casualty, workers' compensation, life, and health insurance lines held a significant portion of the insurance industry's market share nationwide. In addition, we interviewed the state workers' compensation insurance funds for New York and California, which serve as insurers of last resort for employers that cannot find workers' compensation coverage in the private market. Collectively, the private insurers and state funds held the following shares of the markets, by line of insurance:

- 16 percent of the commercial property/casualty insurance market,
- 34 percent of the homeowners insurance market,
- 38 percent of the workers' compensation insurance market,
- 18 percent of the life insurance market, and
- 13 percent of the health insurance market.[61]

In addition, market shares for the private market insurers were among the highest in six states with localities considered by the Insurance Services Office (ISO)—a national organization that prepares insurance rate (price) recommendations and related policies for property/casualty insurers—to be at higher risk for terrorist events (including NBCR events). These insurers usually numbered among the top five insurance providers for their respective lines of insurance in these six states. Depending on the competitiveness of the state market for each insurance line, this market share generally represented anywhere from 2 to 30 percent of the local market. For commercial property/casualty insurance, we also interviewed three specialty insurers, recommended to us by insurance brokers. Specialty insurers are not regulated by state insurance departments but provide stand-alone terrorism insurance coverage that may or may not include NBCR risks.

Finally, to learn more about the availability of NBCR reinsurance coverage, we interviewed representatives of three reinsurers that provide insurance for insurers in the commercial property/casualty market and the group life market, including one reinsurer that focuses its coverage on specific risks such as NBCR events. Two of the reinsurers, as measured by revenue, are among the top three reinsurers in the United States.

To identify state requirements regarding NBCR coverage, we met with and received documentation from the National Association of Insurance Commissioners (NAIC) for a national regulatory perspective as well as insurance regulators in California, New York, and the District of Columbia for individual states' regulations. We selected these states and the District of Columbia because they were among the jurisdictions that have localities considered at high risk for terrorist attacks. Representatives of NAIC were able to provide us with all of the states' legal requirements for property/casualty insurers' coverage of fire following events; however, NAIC did not collect information that would allow us to determine a state's requirements for coverage of NBCR events in workers' compensation, life, and health insurance. State regulators in California, New York, and the District of Columbia provided us with information about their requirements for NBCR coverage for life and health policies issued in their respective states. We gathered information on state workers' compensation requirements for providing NBCR coverage and for pricing this coverage from the National Council on Compensation Insurance—representing 34 states including the District of Columbia—and from workers' compensation rating boards and researchers in New York and California. In the time frames of our study, we could not review all of the state requirements for each of the lines of insurance included in our study. Therefore, for circumstances in which NAIC could not provide us specific state requirements, we relied on national trade associations or information provided by national insurance carriers, particularly for requirements for life and health insurance.

To learn about permissible policy exclusions, we met with ISO and reviewed their standard policies (forms) for commercial property, general liability, and homeowners insurance, including terrorism endorsements. While individual insurer's use of these forms may vary, ISO's forms contain standard policy language. We identified language in these policies that could address issues related to NBCR events, including the nuclear hazard exclusion and the pollution exclusion. We also obtained information about factors that could affect the interpretation of ISO forms from insurers and insurance brokers. In addition, we identified examples of court cases involving disputes over language pertaining to the pollution exclusion in insurance contracts.

Interviews with insurance experts and representatives of three major rating agencies provided additional perspective on insurer willingness to offer NBCR coverage. We selected insurance experts from academia based on their knowledge of insuring for catastrophes, including terrorist acts. We met with representatives of three rating agencies that provide ratings on insurers' financial strength and abilities to meet ongoing obligations to policyholders.

To learn more about supply and demand for NBCR insurance in the commercial property/casualty industry, we reviewed the U.S. Department of the Treasury's (Treasury) 2005 "*Report to Congress, Assessment: The Terrorism Risk Insurance Act of 2002*" and discussed the findings with Treasury staff responsible for its contents. In this report, Treasury reports on results from a series of surveys of commercial property/casualty insurers and policyholders. One survey asked insurers whether they wrote coverage for terrorism risks and whether they wrote any policies that included coverage for any one of the NCBR risks. Another survey asked policyholders from a range of industries whether they purchased NBCR terrorism risk coverage and if not, asked them to identify the reasons. We were limited in our ability to use policyholders' reported purchase rates for NBCR coverage as a signal for approximating overall demand because of the low response rates to these questions. Because a number of surveyed policyholders did not provide this information, there is a risk that those who did not respond differed from those who did, which could lead to bias in the survey results.

To supplement Treasury's data on demand for NBCR coverage in the commercial property/casualty insurance market, we reviewed surveys of the terrorism insurance market conducted by Marsh—a large insurance broker—in 2005 and 2006 as well as by Moody's, a rating agency, in 2005.[62] We also interviewed three risk managers from large companies who purchase commercial property/casualty insurance policies in the real estate, hospitality, and transportation industries, and interviewed representatives of two national associations representing a range of consumers and commercial businesses. The information from both the surveys and the interviews about the availability of NBCR coverage is limited to the specific brokerage clients and individual companies, and cannot be generalized to all policyholders in the United States. Nonresponse rates and other sources of potential error also may limit the use of data from these two surveys.

RELATED GAO PRODUCTS

Insurance Sector Preparedness: Insurers Appear Prepared to Recover Critical Operations Following Potential Terrorist Attacks, but Some Issues Warrant Further Review. GAO-06-85. Washington, D.C.: November 18, 2005.

Catastrophe Risk: U.S. and European Approaches to Insure Natural Catastrophe and Terrorism Risks. GAO-05-199. Washington, D.C.: February 28, 2005.

Terrorism Insurance: Effects of the Terrorism Risk Insurance Act of 2002. GAO-04-806T. Washington, D.C.: May 18, 2004.

Terrorism Insurance: Effects of the Terrorism Risk Insurance Act of 2002. GAO-04-720T. Washington, D.C.: April 28, 2004.

Terrorism Insurance: Implementation of the Terrorism Risk Insurance Act of 2002. GAO-04-307. Washington, D.C.: April 23, 2004.

Catastrophe Insurance Risks: Status of Efforts to Securitize Natural Catastrophe and Terrorism Risk. GAO-03-1033. Washington, D.C.: September 24, 2003.

Catastrophe Insurance Risks: The Role of Risk-Linked Securities and Factors Affecting Their Use. GAO-02-941. Washington, D.C.: September 24, 2002.

Terrorism Insurance: Rising Uninsured Exposure to Attacks Heightens Potential Economic Vulnerabilities. GAO-02-472T. Washington, D.C.: February 27, 2002.

Terrorism Insurance: Alternative Programs for Protecting Insurance Consumers. GAO-02-199T. Washington, D.C.: October 24, 2001.
Terrorism Insurance: Alternative Programs for Protecting Insurance Consumers. GAO-02-175T. Washington, D.C.: October 24, 2001.

GAO'S MISSION

The Government Accountability Office, the audit, evaluation and investigative arm of Congress, exists to support Congress in meeting its constitutional responsibilities and to help improve the performance and accountability of the federal government for the American people. GAO examines the use of public funds; evaluates federal programs and policies; and provides analyses, recommendations, and other assistance to help Congress make informed oversight, policy, and funding decisions. GAO's commitment to good government is reflected in its core values of accountability, integrity, and reliability.

END NOTES

[1] Pub. L. No. 107-297, 116 Stat. 2322 (Nov. 26, 2002), *codified at* 15 U.S.C. § 6701 note.
[2] Emmett J. Vaughan and Therese Vaughan, *Fundamentals of Risk and Insurance*, 9th ed. (Hoboken, N. J.: John Wiley & Sons: 2003).
[3] From an insurance company perspective, a catastrophe is one that has the potential to cause severe losses to an insurance company relative to its available financial resources.
[4] Employers may cover employees for work-related injuries, illness, and death by purchasing an insurance policy from a company licensed by the state, or employers may self-insure.
[5] For more information on TRIA, see GAO, *Terrorism Insurance: Implementation of the Terrorism Risk Insurance Act of 2002,* GAO-04-307 (Washington, D.C.: Apr. 23, 2004).
[6] For purposes of TRIA, "property and casualty insurance" includes commercial lines of property/casualty insurance, including workers' compensation and directors and officers' liability insurance. It does not include other types of insurance such as federal crop insurance, medical malpractice insurance, health or life insurance, commercial automobile insurance, burglary and theft insurance, professional liability insurance or farm owners multiple peril insurance. 15 U.S.C. § 6701 note (Pub. L. No. 107-297, § 102(12)).
[7] TRIA defines "make available" to mean that insurers subject to TRIA must offer coverage for insured losses arising from certified terrorist events and that the coverage not differ materially from the terms, amounts, and limitations applicable to other types of coverage.
[8] Pub. L. No. 109-144, 119 Stat. 2660 (Dec. 22, 2005).
[9] For our description of the elements of an insurable risk, we primarily relied on *Fundamentals of Risk and Insurance*. In addition, we consulted other insurance references.
[10] As described in GAO, *U.S. Postal Service: Better Guidance Is Needed to Ensure an Appropriate Response to Anthrax Contamination*, GAO-04-239 (Washington, D.C.: Sept. 9, 2004), the first cases of bioterrorism anthrax in the United States occurred in September and October 2001, when at least four letters containing anthrax spores were mailed to news media personnel and two U.S. Senators. In addition, as indicated in *Combating Terrorism: Need for Comprehensive Threat and Risk Assessments of Chemical and Biological Attacks*, GAO/NSIAD-99-163 (Washington, D.C.: Sept. 14, 1999), a limited number of incidents involving biological agents, including the contamination of salad bars in local restaurants with salmonella poisoning by the Rajneeshee religious cult, have occurred in the United States.
[11] We contacted insurance experts from academia, including the University of California (Berkeley), Drake University, University of Pennsylvania, Santa Clara University, Georgia State University, as well as the American Academy of Actuaries, and RAND (with expertise in both insurance and national security).
[12] AHIP, July 3, 2003, letter to Office of Microeconomic Analysis, U.S. Department of the Treasury (Treasury).
[13] GAO, *Risk Management: Further Refinements Needed to Assess Risks and Prioritize Protective Measures at Ports and Other Critical Infrastructure* GAO-06-91 (Washington, D.C.: Dec. 15, 2005).
[14] American Academy of Actuaries, April 21, 2006, letter to the President's Working Group on Financial Markets; public comment record, U.S. Department of the Treasury; and Insurance Information Institute, *Terrorism*

Insurance and the United States Government (New York, New York: September 2004). In addition, the Congressional Budget Office (CBO) also noted that terrorism models are hampered not only by a lack of data but also by the absence of an established "theory" of terrorist attacks. CBO, *Federal Terrorism Reinsurance: An Update* (Washington, D.C.: January 2005).

[15] Congressional Research Service, *Terrorism: The New Occupational Hazard,* Order Code RL31387 (Washington, D.C.: Jul. 23, 2002). As noted in this chapter, most of the direct victims of terrorism in the United States in recent years have been people at work, whether those in the World Trade Center or the Pentagon, or victims of anthrax transmitted through the mail.

[16] Statement by American Academy of Actuaries' TRIA Subgroup on Extending or Replacing the Terrorism Risk Insurance Act of 2002, December 1, 2005. The Academy presented this conclusion—that the insurance industry would be impaired by an NBCR attack—based on the assumption that TRIA would be allowed to expire.

[17] While rating agency representatives reported that their agencies have considered the exposure of commercial property/casualty insurers to terrorism generally, none reported that their agencies specifically analyzed exposure to NBCR risks.

[18] See GAO, *Catastrophic Risks: U.S. and European Approaches to Insure Natural Catastrophe and Terrorism Risks*, GAO-05-199 (Washington, D.C.: Feb. 28, 2005) for a description of how insurers use modeling firms to estimate the financial consequences of various natural catastrophe scenarios.

[19] Insurance Information Institute, *Terrorism Insurance and the United States Government* (New York, N.Y.: September 2004).

[20] See GAO-06-91. We concluded that the assessments of selected federal agencies were limited in terms of including information on the relative probability of various threat scenarios. The assessments were limited in their reliability and completeness in part because coordination was needed with the intelligence community.

[21] American Academy of Actuaries, August 2, 2005, letter to the Honorable Richard Baker, Chairman, Subcommittee on Capital Markets, Insurance and Government Sponsored Enterprises, Committee on Financial Services, U.S. House of Representatives.

[22] See appendix I for a description of the insurance experts, insurers, and reinsurers we selected to interview.

[23] From U.S. Department of the Treasury, *"Report to Congress: Assessment: The Terrorism Risk Insurance Act of 2002,"* (Washington, D.C.: Jun. 30, 2005). Treasury reported on the market for terrorism insurance in 2005, using data collected in 2003 and 2004.

[24] According to Treasury, the overall amount of coverage for any of the NBCR events was the same for 2003 and 2004, with an increase in the number of large insurers reporting coverage for NBCR events. The nonresponse rate for this part of the study was 16 percent in 2003 and 9 percent in 2004. Percentages given do not include workers' compensation coverage.

[25] Specialty insurers, also called surplus lines insurers, are not licensed or admitted to generally conduct business in a state but nevertheless are allowed to write insurance in a state under certain circumstances, such as providing insurance for special risks or with terms and conditions having special flexibility.

[26] According to the American Academy of Actuaries, losses for a large NBCR event in both commercial property/casualty and workers' compensation could be substantial. Loss estimates obtained by the Academy indicate that a large NBCR event in a densely populated area could cause total insured losses of $158.3 billion for commercial property, $14.4 billion for general liability, and $483.7 billion for workers' compensation. American Academy of Actuaries, April 21, 2006, letter to the President's Working Group on Financial Markets; public comment record, U.S. Department of the Treasury.

[27] Representatives of the insurers we interviewed said that although TRIA would cover a portion of their losses, the percentage mandated by law for insurer payments represented a sizeable portion of their capital. Under TRIA, insurers affected by a certified terrorist event would currently pay a deductible of 17.5 percent of earned premium in addition to paying 10 percent of the insured losses exceeding the deductible. This is an increase from the deductible amounts in previous years (7 percent in 2003, 10 percent in 2004, and 15 percent in 2005), and less than the 20 percent deductible that they would be responsible for paying in 2007. Treasury also noted the impact of company-specific deductibles in its 2005 report, stating that the deductible may confer an advantage to smaller insurers and insurers writing in single TRIA-eligible lines. Moreover, insurers will be responsible for covering 15 percent of the insured losses exceeding the deductible in 2007. *See* 15 U.S.C. § 6701 note (Pub. L. No. 107-297, §§ 102(7) and 103(e)(1)(A)). As a business strategy, insurers we interviewed had decided to limit their exposure by limiting the amount of business they wrote for NBCR risks.

[28] Litigation remains a concern to representatives of a property/casualty insurer and reinsurer we interviewed because of what has occurred with other terrorist acts. To illustrate, property/casualty insurers were involved in lawsuits related to the 1993 bombing of the World Trade Center as late as November 2005.

[29] Standard Insurance Services Office (ISO) policy contracts state that insurers will not pay for any loss or damage from "nuclear reaction or radiation, or radioactive contamination, however caused." ISO is a national rating organization for the property/casualty insurance industry that develops standardized

policy language designed to be in compliance with regulatory requirements. According to an NAIC representative, regulators have allowed commercial property/casualty insurers to exclude nuclear risks because insurance coverage for nuclear events falls under the Price-Anderson Act, Pub. L. No. 85-256, 71 Stat. 576 (Sept. 2, 1957), codified at 42 U.S.C. §§ 2039, 2210.

[30] After September 11 and prior to the passage of TRIA, ISO created terrorism exclusions with specific references to the dispersal of nuclear or radioactive material and the release of biological or chemical materials. Under TRIA, commercial property/casualty insurers are required to "make available" the same coverage as they did prior to September 11. Because of this, insurance industry representatives told us that insurers have relied on other long-standing exclusions written into standard contracts to limit their exposure to NBCR events.

[31] As of June 28, 2006, according to NAIC, these states were California, Georgia, Hawaii, Illinois, Iowa, Maine, Massachusetts, Missouri, New Jersey, New York, North Carolina, Oregon, Pennsylvania, Washington, West Virginia, and Wisconsin. According to NAIC, since September 11, insurers have tried to limit fire following exposure by lobbying state legislatures to amend standard fire laws so that insurers would not be responsible for fire losses resulting from terrorism. Based upon the information NAIC provided, the number of states that have made such amendments has increased from the last time we reported on terrorism insurance, from seven states in 2004 to 12 in 2006. (See GAO-04-307.) The remaining 22 states and the District of Columbia, according to NAIC, did not have standard fire policies.

[32] GAO has ongoing work in this area.

[33] CBO, *Federal Terrorism Reinsurance: An Update* (Washington, D.C.: January 2005).

[34] As described in GAO, *Capital Hill Anthrax Incident: EPA's Cleanup Was Successful: Opportunities Exist to Enhance Contract Oversight*, GAO-03-686 (Washington, D.C.: Jun. 4, 2003), letters containing a powdered form of anthrax were mailed to members of the news media and congressional leaders, resulting in five deaths and a costly decontamination process.

[35] Treasury reports that 20 percent or fewer policyholders responded to its survey. In addition, Treasury only surveyed policyholders about purchasing NBCR coverage for commercial property/casualty lines. g

[36] The information on demand for terrorism coverage comes from the 2006 Marsh MarketWatch report, published by a large commercial insurance broker using data from more than 2,000 companies, representing two-thirds of their clients.

[37] Captives are special-purpose insurance companies set up by commercial businesses to self-insure risks arising from the owners' business activities. Captives may be insurers under TRIA and therefore may be eligible for payments for losses related to certified NBCR events.

[38] The guidance NAIC issued, termed a "model bulletin," also stated they did not believe terrorism exclusions were needed in personal property/casualty insurance (including homeowners' insurance policies). See NAIC Model Bulletin (Dec. 21, 2001) addressing exclusions related to acts of terrorism, personal lines property/casualty coverage, life insurance, health insurance, and workers' compensation.

[39] American Academy of Actuaries, Public Policy Monograph, *P/C Terrorism Insurance Coverage: Where Do We Go Post-Terrorism Risk Insurance Act?* (Washington, D.C.: May 2004). In addition, Pennsylvania is an exception to this general rule because that state allows insurers to exclude losses from disability or death resulting from military activities or enemy sabotage. *See* 77 P.S. § 1209 and 77 P.S. § 431.

[40] NCCI helps insurers develop and file loss costs and rates in 33 states and the District of Columbia.

[41] NCCI developed the terrorism surcharge using information from a modeling firm on potential losses to workers' compensation lines. The surcharge is applicable to 36 states—2 more than the number of states where NCCI files loss costs or rates. However, this surcharge was not developed for non-NCCI states, a group which includes some states with localities considered to be at higher risk for terrorism attacks—including California, New York, and Texas.

[42] The Rating Board determines workers' compensation rates in New York.

[43] As we previously noted, insurers use historical information from a large number of occurrences to determine potential future losses. In addition, workers' compensation insurers that underwrite in California told us that even if they could charge higher prices to specifically cover NBCR risks, they could not use these funds to establish separate reserves to cover potential losses until after an event had occurred.

[44] In addition, GAO has reported on difficulties in identifying whether chemical agents were the source of long-term illness. See GAO, *Gulf War Illnesses: DOD's Conclusions about U.S. Troops' Exposure Cannot Be Adequately Supported*, GAO-04-159 (Washington, D.C.: Jun. 1, 2004).

[45] Workers' compensation insurance only would cover injury or illness that occurred or was contracted on the job or when the employee was acting within the scope of employment.

[46] In other words, workers' compensation insurers charge different rates, depending on the risk of death or injury by occupation, but they must charge the same statewide rate for occupation regardless of geographic location. For example, workers' compensation insurers charge higher rates for roofers than for clerical staff. However, according to NCCI representatives, employers pay the same rate for a roofer in an area considered at greater risk for a terrorism attack as they pay for a roofer in an area considered less at risk.

[47] The New York State Insurance Fund and the State Compensation Insurance Fund of California are both insurers of last resort for employers that otherwise cannot find workers' compensation insurance in their respective states. See appendix I for information about their market share nationwide.

[48] Although neither NAIC nor the American Council of Life Insurers could tell us about requirements across all states related to exclusions for terrorism and NBCR risks, NAIC told us that many states allow life insurers to exclude losses from an act of war. California state regulatory officials told us that they did not include terrorism within the definition of an act of war.

[49] California regulatory officials told us that not all life products are subject to regulatory review, and therefore some forms sold by life insurers in California could exclude NBCR risks.

[50] For example, according to one insurer, a group life insurer might anticipate three or four deaths per 1,000 people through ordinary causes of death, but an incident that caused more than four deaths per 1,000 would require additional funds beyond what the insurer anticipated.

[51] In general, when insurers become insolvent and cannot pay their claims, state insolvency guarantee funds compensate members of the public who suffer losses, although the policyholders may bear part of the losses themselves.

[52] According to a model developed for the American Academy of Actuaries, a large NBCR event could cause widespread casualties resulting in insured losses to life insurers of $82 billion. See footnote 26.

[53] NAIC also does not track state requirements regarding the coverage of NBCR events in health insurance policies across the states. California regulatory officials told us that some health insurance forms could exclude NBCR coverage if such a form were not disapproved by the state within 30 days of filing.

[54] American Academy of Actuaries, December 2002, Public Policy Monograph, *Group and Health Coverage in the Wake of September 11*. The Academy specifically noted that a biological, chemical, or radiological attack could spread illness for extended periods. In addition, we have noted that the symptoms from some biological agents easily could be confused with other, more common illnesses. See GAO/NSIAD-99-163.

[55] Unlike workers' compensation insurance, health insurers with whom we spoke told us that their policies covered medical treatments for current illnesses or injuries, regardless of when the person got sick or hurt.

[56] The capabilities and availability of public health personnel and medicines or vaccines could affect the scope of damage and casualties, as we have previously noted in reports on the preparedness of public health agencies and health care organizations for biological attacks. See GAO, *Infectious Disease Outbreaks: Bioterrorism Preparedness Efforts Have Improved Public Health Response Capacity, but Gaps Remain,* GAO-03-654T, (Washington, D.C.: Apr. 9, 2003) and GAO, *Bioterrorism: Preparedness Varied across State and Local Jurisdictions*, GAO-03-373 (Washington, D.C.: Apr. 7, 2003).

[57] Emmett J. Vaughan and Therese Vaughan, *Fundamentals of Risk and Insurance,* 9th ed. (Hoboken, N.J.: John Wiley & Sons, 2003).

[58] From an insurance perspective, a catastrophe is one that has the potential to cause severe losses to an insurance company relative to its available financial resources.

[59] *Cat Modeling 2006: Shifting Paradigms*, presented by the Reinsurance Association of America, Tampa, Fla.: February 2006.

[60] The Insurance Information Institute provides information and analysis of insurance topics and collects data on insurance premiums and market shares for individual states as well as for the entire United States. Moody's Investors Services, as part of its Special Comment on insurers' exposure to terrorist risks, published information about workers' compensation insurers' premiums and market share.

[61] All of the information about market share data came from the Insurance Information Institute, with the exception of workers' compensation insurance, which came from Moody's Special Comment on Terrorism Insurance in 2005. While the state funds only underwrite workers' compensation in their respective states, Moody's calculated their marketshare based on a percentage of total premiums written nationwide.

[62] These studies were the *Marsh MarketWatch Report: 2006 and Moody's Special Comment Letter on Terrorism Insurance: 2005.*

Chapter Sources

The following chapters have been previously published:

Chapter 1 is an edited, reformatted and augmented version of a Congressional Research Service Report for Congress publication, Publication RL34219, updated January 2008.

Chapter 2 is an edited, reformatted and augmented version of a Congressional Research Service Report for Congress publication, Publication RL34025, updated November 2007.

Chapter 3 is an edited, reformatted and augmented version of a United States Government Accountability Office Report to Congress, Publication GAO-09-39, dated December 2008.

Chapter 4 is an edited, reformatted and augmented version of a United States Government Accountability Office Report to Congress, Publication GAO-08-1057, dated September 2008.

Chapter 5 is an edited, reformatted and augmented version of a United States Government Accountability Office Report to the Chairman, Committee on Finance, House of Representatives. Publication GAO-06-1081, dated September 2006.

INDEX

9

A

B

C

D

I

J

K

L

M

N

S